DATE DUE

last chk-in 2/

2/94

Execution Eve

Execution Eve

William J. Buchanan

New Horizon Press
Far Hills, New Jersey

Copyright Acknowledgments

The author and publisher gratefully acknowledge permission to quote from the following copyrighted material:

"To Kill or Not to Kill" by Allan Trout. Copyright © *The Courier-Journal*. Used with permission.

Copyright © 1993 by William J. Buchanan

Requests for permission should be addressed to:
New Horizon Press
P.O. Box 669
Far Hills, NJ 07931

Buchanan, William J.
        Execution Eve

Library of Congress Catalog Card Number: 92-60568

ISBN: 0-88282-121-0
New Horizon Press

Manufactured in the U.S.A.

1997 1996 1995 1994 1993 / 5 4 3 2 1

Dedicated to the memory of my father

Acknowledgments

I wish to acknowledge a debt of gratitude to my father, Warden W. Jesse Buchanan, who made his personal papers available to me and answered myriad questions with candor; to Governor A. B. "Happy" Chandler, Deputy Warden Porter Lady, Death House Supervisor John Rankin and Columnist Allan Trout who added invaluable details during my research; to my mother, Margaret Kagy Buchanan, and sister, Margaret Baldwin Clements, for their contributions about Frog Island, and other key events; to Father Thomas Libs, who related events not a matter of public or church records; and to the three convicted murderers, Thomas Penney, Raymond Baxter, and Robert Anderson, who shared intensely personal recollections and thoughts with me during the final days, hours and minutes of their lives.

Thanks also to Clara Wiedemann, Frances Baccus, O. Thomas Bell, William Biggs, A. Waller Clements, Hugh and Mary Louise Greene, Porter Lady, Jr., James Park, Jr., Frankie Thomas, Jim Thomas, Odell Walker, and others who wish to remain anonymous, for their help during my more recent research for the book.

Finally, a special thanks to my wife, Milli, for her encouragement and priceless assistance during the final composition of the manuscript.

Author's Note

My original research into this story was for a segment for my college thesis, *Men Facing Death: A Study of Capital Punishment in America* (University of Louisville, 1950). It was only recently, following an upsurge of legal executions in the United States, that I decided to expand those original notes into a book.

Much of what occurs in the narrative to follow I witnessed firsthand. The remainder is based on public accounts, trial records, private papers, and incidents that were related to me by those involved, including the three condemned men central to the story. In attempting to recreate actual events and dialogue I have used a reasonable literary licence within narrow confines of truth and credibility. Nonetheless, all scenes are recounted as closely as possible to how I witnessed them or how they were told to me.

Oh, how well do I remember the night Poor Willie died,
The flowers lay lowly drooping in the mud,
And the warden had agreed that to suit Poor Willie's need,
He would stop the circulation of his blood.

—Underground ditty,
Kentucky State Prison

Execution
Eve

1

Raymond S. "Willie" Baxter lay clutching his blue woolen blanket close beneath his chin, gazing up through the barred window high in the rear wall of his cell. For twelve months that tiny window had provided Willie's only view of the outside world. Through it he had watched the seasons change, had gazed at the stars long into the night, and—his greatest pleasure—had listened to the songbirds that nested in the towering black gum tree in the prison yard. Willie liked birds.

This February morning the sky was leaden. A mantle of low-hanging clouds had induced a chill in the usually mild pre-spring Kentucky weather. Worse, it had blotted out the sun. That annoyed Willie, for he and the sun had conspired in a pastime that delighted him. On better days the golden rays filtering through the bars cast a latticework of shadows that inched their way across the barren cement floor and slowly climbed the opposite wall. Willie watched the shadows intently, trying to guess the time of day as they made their slow progression. Despite months of trying, he'd never mastered it—not the way Tom had. Tom could predict the hour within two minutes of the actual time registered on the face of the large Seth Thomas clock mounted above the green-and-tan door directly across the corridor from Willie's cell.

Sun or not, Willie had slept late this morning. The muted hubbub of sounds rising from the main prison yard just below his window told him that the day was well underway. Captain Rankin had let him sleep late. Captain Rankin did that often, for Willie never ate breakfast anyway. But there'd be coffee, rich and freshly brewed by Captain Rankin in his office, with plenty of sugar and canned milk to stir in it. Death house inmates were the only convicts allowed unlimited amounts of sugar and milk for their coffee. Even on the outside, Willie had heard, few people in these wartime days of 1943 could obtain unlimited amounts of sugar and milk—even if they could find coffee. Willie smiled at the thought. Captain Rankin was good to him.

Willie kicked back the cover, stood, and stretched long and hard beside his bed. A small man, he stood only five-and-a-half feet tall and weighed 115 pounds. He was twenty-eight. Beneath a thick shock of sandy hair, which on most days he brushed straight back without a part, his pock-marked face, deeply sunken cheeks, prominent off-center nose, and melancholy brown eyes gave him the look of an emaciated weasel. His ever-sallow complexion, accentuated by months of incarceration, extended over his entire body. On the inside of his arms, at the bend of his elbows, an unsightly patch of long-healed scar tissue bore mute testimony to a life of drug addiction.

Standing there nude, as he always slept, Willie was nonetheless comfortable. The death house, intolerable during the scorching summer months, was pleasantly steam-heated during colder weather. He stepped to the opposite corner of his cell and urinated into a lidless steel commode fixed to the wall. When he finished, he pushed the handle and watched the amber waste swirl and disappear down the drain. Flush toilets, too, were luxuries for condemned men only. Convicts in the general line had only wooden slop pails, which they carried out each morning to be emptied at the prison sewage plant, rinsed with Lysol, then hung on wooden pegs to dry for use the following night. Seldom did an inmate get the same pail twice.

Willie grabbed his khaki trousers and lightweight denim shirt from the foot of his bed and slipped them on. His inmate identification number was stenciled in bold white numerals across the shirt pocket and again in even larger numbers across the back. He sat on the edge of the bed and picked up a pair of thin white cotton socks that lay wadded in a ball on the floor. He pulled on the socks, then stepped into a pair of frayed corduroy house slippers. He hadn't been outside the confines of the death house since his arrival a year before. Every third day he was escorted by two guards to Captain Rankin's office at the head of the corridor for a shave from a convict barber. Every third week he received a hair trim, every Monday a bath. During all those months he hadn't worn shoes, underwear, or a belt. The absence of a belt was a death house rule. The foregoing of shoes and underwear was Willie's choice. The wear on his slippers was the result of a daily one-mile walk, five hundred trips wall-to-wall, back and forth across the length of his cell.

After dressing, Willie pulled a pack of Chesterfield cigarettes from his shirt pocket and shoved one in his mouth. He had seldom smoked ready-mades before coming to prison. They were too expensive. On the outside he smoked Bull Durham, five cents a bag, including twenty sheets of roll-your-own paper. Here it was different. Churches and other charitable groups vied for the privilege of providing permissible items to condemned men, and cigarettes, purchased from the tightly controlled prison canteen, were high on the list. Cigarettes purchased from sources outside the prison were not allowed.

Willie patted his pockets and located a match folder. It was empty. Shit.

He went to the front of his cell and pushed his face against the bars. "Archie"—his voice had the timbre of a clarinet with a bad reed—"gotta match?"

No reply.

"Archie?"

This time a clear baritone voice answered from the end cell down the corridor to Willie's right. "He's not there, Willie."

"Hey, Tom!" Willie said. "What's with Archie?"

"They moved him to Block Three early this morning," Thomas Penney replied. "Gray, too. There's no one left down here but you, me, and Bob."

"How come?" Willie asked.

"Think about it, Willie."

There was no response.

"We're the stars of the show tonight, Willie," Tom explained. "This place will be crawling with reporters all day, and Big Jess doesn't want two more cons down here confusing things."

Willie pondered this. Slow of wit, he found it difficult at times to follow Tom's oblique way of explaining things. After a moment he grasped Toms meaning. "Hey . . . Governor Johnson's not gonna let that happen, huh, Tom? Not all three of us on the same night. One of them reporters that was down here yesterday . . . that guy from Paducah . . . he told me it'd never go down like that."

"That guy from Paducah's not the governor, Willie." Tom's voice was caring, like that of a concerned parent explaining things to a confused child. Talking to Willie was like that sometimes. "Yes, Johnson *will* let it happen. Tonight. Prepare yourself for that, Willie."

Just then, another voice thundered from the opposite end of the death house. "Penney, you miserable asshole, clam up! Willie, you hear me?"

"Yeah . . . I hear you, Bob."

"Don't listen to that crazy son of a bitch, Willie. He's been aching for months to get his ass fried, but that don't mean your number's up. Mine sure as hell ain't. It won't happen. You listen to me, Willie. *It won't happen.*"

"Morning, Bob." Tom spoke up so his voice would carry

through the corridor. "Didn't know you were speaking to me these days."

"I'll be speaking to you plenty before this day's out, you no-good bastard," Robert Anderson replied. "So will my lawyers. This rap's not going down like you set it up. You can bet your ass on that."

Tom looked at the clock across the hall. It was 9:00 A.M. "You've got fifteen hours left, Bob. I advise you to use it to make peace with God."

"You can stow that shit, too."

In his office across the corridor from the cells, Death House Supervisor John Rankin shook his head as he listened to yet another acrimonious exchange between Anderson and Penney. Rankin was a huskily built man with thick gray hair and Brillo-pad eyebrows that no barber dared touch. Although his pay scale reflected the rank of a captain of the guards, the only supervisory duty he had over other prison officials was on the evening of an execution, when a guard detail was assigned to death house duty. His usual dress for his job was everyday civilian clothes, but on this day he was immaculately attired in the dark blue uniform denoting his rank. From the beginning of his employment at the penitentiary as assistant death house supervisor twenty-three years before, his only wards had been condemned men. Two years later, when he was promoted to fill the position of the retiring death house supervisor, he began the full-uniform ritual on the final day of a condemned man's life. He considered it an act of common decency. His compassion for his charges had earned him sincere respect from all inmates at the institution.

Captain Rankin rose from his desk, took three heavy white china mugs from the cupboard, and filled them with hot coffee from a pot on his office stove. He stirred two heaping teaspoons of sugar and a couple of ounces of canned milk into one cup. The other two he left black. He put the cups on a tray and stepped across the corridor to Bob Anderson's cell.

"This isn't a day for that sort of talk, Bob," he admonished. He handed one of the black coffees through the bars.

Thirty-eight-year-old Bob Anderson looked anything but what he was—a convicted killer. Of average height, stockily built with a double chin and distinct paunch, he had not, as had his two associates, lost weight during incarceration. His round, almost cherubic face usually shone with good humor. It was only when talking to or discussing Tom Penney that his dark eyes flashed with anger.

He took the coffee. "Thanks, Captain Rankin. No offense meant to you or anyone else except that bastard at the end of the hall."

Captain Rankin let it pass and stepped to Willie's cell. He handed the sugared and creamed coffee through the bars. "Here's your morning milkshake, son."

Willie smiled at the longstanding joke between him and Captain Rankin. He took the cup. It was the only thing he ever took for breakfast. Pearl didn't like that about him, he remembered. She always tried to get him to eat a bowl of cereal, or at least a piece of toast, with his coffee. The thought made him sad. He didn't want to think about Pearl anymore. He tried to banish her from his mind by concentrating again on the limited view beyond the window.

At the last cell Captain Rankin handed the remaining black coffee through the bars. "Looks like you're catching up on your correspondence, Tom."

"Yes sir." Tom rose from his desk and took the coffee. "Thank you, Captain."

Captain Rankin stepped to the center of the corridor, where he could be seen by all three men. How much easier it would be, he thought, if they were kept in adjoining cells. But the separation was the warden's orders, and Captain Rankin didn't question orders.

He cleared his throat. "Tom . . . Willie . . . Bob"—he looked at each man as he spoke their names—"there's going to be a lot of people showing up here today. Lawyers, reporters, preachers. They'll surely want to talk to you. Warden Buchanan says that's your decision. As you know, he usually invites reporters to come with him when he makes the final reading of the warrants. If you want to talk to them afterward, fine. If you don't, that's fine, too. The warden has instructed me to respect your decision in the matter."

He moved closer to the green-and-tan door.

"Now, since you've been here you've seen eight men go through this door. You know the routine. And you know I'll be here for you. If there's anything you want, anything I can do, just ask."

Bob Anderson called out, "How about a one-way ticket to Louisville, Captain?"

Rankin chuckled at the death house humor. "Out of my jurisdiction, Bob. I'm afraid the only person who can do that for you now is Governor Johnson."

"Not true," Bob retorted. "There's someone else can do it. *You listening, Penney?* Tell the captain how you railroaded me. You and your Holy-Joe act about being so concerned for your soul. You may have everybody else around here conned, but you ain't fooling me one bit. My life's on your soul, Penney, *and we both know why.* And you're going to burn in hell for it unless you come clean in time for Johnson to act. Tell him that, Captain. Talk some sense into his thick skull."

Captain Rankin shook his head and went to his office. He switched on the radio connected to two speakers mounted on the wall across from the cells. A rich baritone voice was singing: *"Heaven . . . I'm in Heaven . . ."*

"Hey, Penney," Bob called. "Hear that? That's the Old Groaner himself. He helped put your ass in this hell-hole, remember? Well, soon as I get sprung I'm going to make a special trip to Hollywood just to shake his hand for that."

Tom ignored the diatribe. Seated at his desk, where he had been since dawn, he leaned back in his chair and listened to the mellow voice of Bing Crosby croon the words to "Cheek to Cheek." It was one of Penney's favorite songs.

The song ended and the announcer introduced another record. Tom Penney turned back to his work. On his desk was a writing tablet, a Watterman fountain pen, a package of Chesterfield cigarettes, and a box of Whitman chocolates, unopened. A shelf above the desk held a dozen well-thumbed books, among them *The Long Way Home* by Robert Benson, *The Following of Christ* by Thomas à Kempis, *The Spiritual Life* by Edgar Brightman, *The Song of Bernadette* by Franz Werfel, and the Catholic Bible. Beneath the shelf, stuck to the wall with tape, was a list of names scrawled in Toms handwriting: *Father George, Father Brian, Sister Robert Ann, Sister Mary Laurentia, Mother.* The first name had been lined through. One letter lay folded on the bed.

He thought of a name not on the list. He sat back and looked toward the cell window and conjured up her image.

Pam. Blithe spirit with the bewitching smile.

He wondered where she was. Had she followed her dream to California? He wished he knew, wished he could write to her and explain the dreadful things she must have read about him by now.

After a moment he turned back to the desk and picked up the pen and started a letter to Father Brian. Before he finished the salutation he laid the pen down. He leaned forward with his elbows on the desk and gripped his head with both hands. He hadn't gone to bed until well after midnight and had tossed fitfully until sunup. It had been that way now for seventeen months, ever since that night of horror in Lexington. For a long while afterward he had avoided sleeping at night, thinking that by napping during the day he could avoid the dream. It was futile, for the dream came not with darkness but with sleep. So he had turned to alcohol. Thereafter, his sleep became drunken stupors. Then, following his capture, the booze ended and once again sleep became terror. This morning, as he had every morning since incarceration, he awakened at dawn with an excruciating headache. *Well,* he thought, *this will be the last.* The ultimate cure to all his bodily ills loomed just on the other side of that green-and-tan door across the hallway, just hours ahead. No more headaches. Indeed, no more sunrises.

His thoughts turned to Bob Anderson, and the throbbing in his head intensified. He got up and stepped over to his bed. He was taller than his companions, standing an even six feet without shoes, with the sinewy build of one who had worked long at physical labor. His ruggedly handsome Nordic features were marred only by a jagged scar extending down his left cheek from below his chestnut hair to his chin. He was thirty-four.

He reached beneath his pillow and retrieved a wooden rosary. The beads were shiny from constant fingering. He grasped the rood tightly in his hands and returned to his desk and looked again at the list of names taped to the wall. Four names remained. Four letters. But it was another letter that obsessed his thoughts at this moment. A fifth and final letter he must write, to a person whose name was not taped there with the rest.

The last and most important letter of his life.

2

As he did each morning at five o'clock when reveille sounded for the inmate population, Warden W. Jesse Buchanan rose from bed in his private apartment on the second floor, administration building, of the Kentucky State Penitentiary. His sleep had been fitful. A subdued glow from the lighted front steps just below his window dimly illuminated the room. Moving quietly, so as not to awaken his wife sleeping in her own bed across the room, he slipped a red silk robe over his pajamas and went down the long hallway to the spacious marbled bathroom that had been designed to accommodate his great size. One of the country's most esteemed wardens, he was by far the largest. Six-feet eight-inches tall, weighing three hundred pounds, he was, in spite of his fifty-nine years, solidly built. His biceps were as large as an average man's thigh. The Kentucky cluster diamond ring he wore, a gift from his wife, measured a full inch in inside diameter. Every article of his clothing except socks, handkerchiefs, and ties was tailored by a clothier in Evansville, Indiana.

After bathing, the warden toweled briskly, then combed his silver hair into a part high on the left side. He would be shaved later that morning in the officers' barber shop by an inmate serving a life sentence for armed robbery.

He detoured back through the hallway for a moment to retrieve a package he had stored in a desk there the day before, then went to the apartment's country-size kitchen. He handed the package to a large black man who was turning sausage patties in a cast-iron skillet atop a coal-burning range. Lucien Greenwell laid down the spatula and wiped his hands on his apron. He took the package and laid it aside near the stove. "Yessir. I'll put 'em on right after breakfast."

Back-to-back, Greenwell stood a half-inch shorter than the warden. But in all other respects of girth and size the two were identical. The package the warden handed his cook that morning contained a new pair of shoes, size 15-EEE, just arrived from a cobbler in Boston. The warden detested new shoes. Lucien would wear them until they were well broken in, then return them. An amusing pastime at the prison was observing Lucien Greenwell's feet for evidence that the warden had purchased a new pair of shoes.

The warden sat down and poured himself a cup of coffee. Lucien brought eggs, sausages, and biscuits to the table, laid two morning newspapers near the warden's plate, then pulled up a chair and sat down. Then, as they had each morning for six years, the warden of Kentucky's maximum security penitentiary and a convict serving life for murder ate the first meal of the day together.

Breakfast finished, the warden put on a pair of horn-rimmed glasses and picked up the first paper. War news dominated the front page. With one son in the Navy and another preparing to enter the Army Air Corps, he read about the German advances in Europe and North Africa with heavy heart.

12

Finishing the lead stories, he thumbed through the following pages looking for the article he knew would be there today. He found it near the bottom of page two. Two columns wide, it read:

MILEY MURDERERS TO DIE TONIGHT
Lexington, Ky. — Barring intervention from Governor Johnson or the courts, a scar-faced carpenter, a burly cafe owner, and a dope-addicted handyman will die tonight in the electric chair at Eddyville. Thomas C. Penney, Robert H. Anderson, and Raymond S. Baxter, convicted for the murders of popular golf star Marion Miley and her mother at the Lexington Country Club in 1941, are slated to begin their walk to death just minutes past midnight tonight.

Subsequent paragraphs described the brutality of the murders, the trials, the previous stays of execution. The final paragraph posed a chilling question:

Is Anderson guilty? Despite the latest ruling from the Court of Appeals, doubts about Robert Anderson's guilt continue to plague legal scholars and some officials close to the case. Anderson's attorneys vow to continue the fight to save their client's life and are planning to meet again with Governor Johnson in Frankfort today.

The warden laid the paper down, removed his heavy glasses, and rubbed his eyes wearily. He'd been thinking about Bob Anderson for days. Indeed, it had ruined his sleep for nights. There were too many unanswered questions about the man's involvement in the killings—too many loose ends. Surely the truth about Bob Anderson would surface some day. But someday might be too late—for both Anderson and himself.

His mind focused on another thought, something that had come to him during the night, though he realized on reflection that he'd been mulling it over for days. Perhaps there *was* a way to determine if Anderson was guilty or innocent before it was too late. It would be risky, controversial, perhaps even unlawful. It would mean reneging on a plan he had formulated earlier with Governor Johnson. But that would be a small price to pay to save the life of a possibly innocent man. He made a mental note to inform the deputy warden of his plan following the morning staff meeting.

He finished his second cup of coffee, folded the papers, and handed them to Lucien to read later. Then he went to his bedroom to finish dressing before going downstairs to his office.

It was going to be a long day.

3

From his office high in the Citizens Bank Building at Fourth and Broadway in Paducah, Kentucky, Thomas S. Waller, senior partner at Waller, Threlkeld & Whitlow, Attorneys at Law, sat facing the window and gazed into the distance beyond the Ohio River, deep in thought. A large man, known for his trademark dark suits and Kentucky Colonel string ties, Waller was renowned as a quick study with penetrating insight. One of the South's most prominent attorneys, his appointment calendar was filled months in advance. Yet he had cancelled all appointments for this day and asked his secretary to hold all calls. After a while he swiveled back to his desk and noted today's date on his calendar pad—Thursday, February 25, 1943. He had circled the date in red months before on the day when Warden Buchanan came to see him in confidence.

For over fifty years Tom Waller and Jess Buchanan had been the closest of friends. They had grown up together in Union County. Each held the other in utmost esteem, each respected the other's opinion. In matters of law, Jess Buchanan always sought Tom Waller's counsel. In matters of politics, Waller usually deferred to Buchanan's instincts. But on that day four months ago when Buchanan came to see his old friend, Waller sensed that there was more to the visit than a question of politics or legal fine points. The warden was in torment.

The two old friends talked for most of the morning. At the end, Tom Waller agreed to honor Buchanan's request: Yes, he would study the Miley Case in detail to try to detect any flaw in the case against Robert Anderson.

Now, Waller pulled a heavy file from his HOLD basket. Compiled from news clippings, court records, and transcribed private conversations, the file was marked MILEY CASE. He had read every word of every document at least a half-dozen times. Still, he decided to spend the remainder of this day doing so again. He opened the file and started at the beginning:

The crime that tormented the warden and occupied Tom Waller occurred during the pre-dawn hours of September 28, 1941. At 4:15 that Sunday morning, J. M. Giles, manager of the Ben Mar Sanatorium in the fashionable northeast section of Lexington, Kentucky, was awakened by the repeated ringing of his doorbell accompanied by faint cries for help. He threw on a robe, went to the front door, and opened it to horror. A woman, barefoot and dressed in a blood-drenched nightgown, took a feeble step inside and collapsed into his arms. Giles recognized her at once. She was Mrs. Elsie Miley, 52, director of the Lexington Country Club just across the highway. Barely able to talk, she gasped out a tale of being beaten, shot, and robbed.

"Marion . . . ," the woman cried, "shot . . . please, get help."

Giles yelled for a member of his staff to summon an ambulance and the police, and began rendering first aid to the stricken woman.

The prestigious Lexington Country Club was situated on lush bluegrass acreage on Paris Pike, three miles from downtown. Fifteen minutes after being notified, Lexington police entered the clubhouse to find wires cut, phones ripped from the walls, and furniture smashed. Upstairs, the door to Mrs. Miley's apartment was splintered from its hinges. Inside was carnage. The entry hallway and bedrooms had been ransacked. In the master bedroom the floor and bed were blood-soaked. At the head of the hallway, officers made a more gruesome discovery: lying dead in a pool of blood, clad in pajamas, was twenty-seven-year-old Marion Miley. She had been shot at close range in the back and again in the top of her head. An autopsy would show that she died at approximately 2:30 A.M. Physicians speculated that her mother had lain in a state of shock for over an hour before acquiring enough strength to make her desperate crawl for help.

Within hours, the murder in Kentucky was headline news throughout the United States and Europe, for Marion Miley was a household name on both sides of the Atlantic.

A winning athlete since age eighteen, Marion had risen steadily through the ranks of female golfers. Along the way she won every major American tournament open to women, garnering a reputation for being "cool under fire—a golfer without nerves." In her early twenties she represented the United States in major European tournaments. Hailed by sportswriters as being on a par with her good friends Patty Berg and "Babe" Didrickson, both of whom she defeated in competition, Marion was officially ranked the number-two woman golfer in the country. She was well on her way to becoming number one. Vivacious, outgoing, and strongly competitive, the pretty brunette star was once asked by a reporter in London how it felt to be ranked among the top women golfers in the world.

She replied, "Why stop with women?"

It was that kind of spirit that endeared her to competitors and fans alike.

As news of Marion's murder spread, golf patrons around the country reacted in shock, then anger. Spearheaded by the game's most famous amateur, Bing Crosby, celebrities by the score contributed generously to the reward for the capture of her killer.

Slipping in and out of consciousness, Elsie Miley whispered a fractured account of what had happened. She had been awakened by the sound of something breaking. Police later determined that she had heard one of the intruders knock over a lamp at the head of the stairs. Then two men burst into her apartment, grabbed her roughly, and demanded to know where she had hidden the money. Before she could reply, one of the men shot her. In a voice so weak that the police detective had to place his ear directly over her mouth, she murmured a meager description of her assailants: two men, one tall and slender, the other shorter and stocky.

Had she seen which one of the men shot Marion? the detective asked.

Mrs. Miley nodded. But before she could speak again, she lapsed into a final coma. On October 1, three days after she had been shot, and seven hours after her daughter's funeral, Elaine Miley died.

With no usable fingerprints found at the scene, investigators combed the Country Club area for any hint as to the killers' identities. For the first couple of days, it was a fruitless search. Then, in rapid succession, two important clues emerged.

Each morning, while most people in Lexington were still sleeping, newsboy Hugh Cramer, 17, rose to deliver papers. The Lexington Country Club was on his route. Between 3:00 and 3:30 A.M. Sunday, he tossed Mrs. Miley's paper onto the stoop of the clubhouse. There were three cars parked in the driveway. He recognized two. One was Mrs. Miley's. The other belonged to her daughter Marion, who, Cramer knew, lived with her mother between tournaments. The third car, standing with its door open, was strange.

At first, Cramer didn't consider the third car unusual. There had been a dance at the club the night before. Sometimes, after a social event, club members would leave their cars and ride home with friends. But as news of the Miley murders spread, Cramer remembered that third car and notified police.

Could he describe the car? police asked.

Like any teenage car buff, Cramer could. It was a 1941 Buick Sedan, two-tone blue and gray. He didn't notice the plates, but was sure he would have had they been from outside Kentucky.

Police released an all-points bulletin on the Buick.

The second clue was even more incriminating. During a questioning, two Lexington men brought in for interrogation told investigators that a couple of weeks earlier, a scar-faced ex-convict they met in a bar tried to enlist them to help rob the Country Club. The ex-con's name: Tom Penney.

Tom Penney was well known to Lexington police. The black-sheep son of a law-abiding family, he had been a troublemaker for years. At sixteen he was sent to reform school for car theft. Paroled, he pulled off a series of minor crimes until, in 1930, he was convicted of the armed robbery of a grocery store during which he shot two men. Following his release he worked around Lexington as a part-time carpenter but could not hold any job for long. Mean and belligerent, he was the principal suspect in several open cases on the police blotter. He was currently out of jail on another parole.

On the heels of the all-points bulletin on the Buick, police issued another on Penney.

The second APB was not necessary.

On October 9, eleven days after the Miley shootings, two police officers in Fort Worth, Texas, parked their patrol car in a vacant lot near an intersection where a number of speeders had been reported. Moments later, a blue-gray Buick with Kentucky plates roared through the four-way stop without slowing. The officers gave chase.

At the first wail of the siren, the speeder pulled to the side. While one officer radioed headquarters, the second approached the parked Buick. The driver was a tall, slender man with a jagged scar across his left cheek. His eyes were bloodshot and his speech was slurred. His drivers license identified him as Thomas Penney of Lexington, Kentucky.

The officer had just started back to the patrol car to check out the drivers license when the second officer replaced the microphone on the dash and stepped out. "We've got a hot one. That's the car in the Miley murders."

Both officers approached the car with their weapons drawn and ordered the driver to step out with his hands up. While one kept Penney covered, the other searched the Buick. From beneath the front seat he withdrew a .38-caliber revolver—loaded and cocked.

Penney's confession was so effusive that it aroused suspicion. As one investigator would later testify, the fleeing Kentuckian was "just too damned eager to talk." He had indeed taken part in the Miley murders, Penney admitted. Without prompting, he named an accomplice: Robert Anderson of Louisville. The Buick, Penney said, belonged to Anderson.

Robert H. Anderson was well-known to the Kentucky officials. Proprietor of a blue-collar Louisville nightclub, The Cat and Fiddle, he was respected by his business associates and patrons alike. On weekends, Louisville swarmed with soldiers on pass from nearby Fort Knox. Anderson ordered his bartenders to serve the boys in uniform drinks at half price, and occasionally to serve one on the house. Among the GIs it was well known that any one of them down on his luck could always count on a sandwich and beer, gratis, at Bob Anderson's place. More than once, Anderson paid the bus fare so that a soldier in danger of being listed AWOL could return to the fort on time.

The personable proprietor also had a dark side to his nature. Quick to anger, he could resort to violence on the slightest provocation. He kept a BB-filled blackjack behind the bar and wasn't hesitant to use it to whip a rowdy customer into line. Once, learning that a local con artist was hustling soldiers in a back room with loaded dice, Anderson beat the man to a bloody pulp and tossed him into the alley behind the club with a warning to never step foot in The Cat and Fiddle again. Neither the con artist nor any of the others who suffered Anderson's wrath dared complain to authorities.

Arrested by Louisville police on the day Penny implicated him, Anderson was indignant. He heatedly denied any involvement in the crime. He admitted knowing Tom Penney from the days the two of them served time together in the state reformatory. Following Penney's latest release from prison, Anderson said, he had helped the ex-con with an occasional odd job and sometimes with an outright grubstake. More recently, Anderson admitted, he had been buying contraband whiskey from Penney, whose latest scam was hijacking delivery trucks serving one or more of the many distilleries around central Kentucky.

Why would Penney falsely accuse him? officers asked.

Anderson had an explanation. In September, he said, Penney arrived at The Cat and Fiddle with twenty cases of scotch. He said he needed a lot of money quick and offered to sell the whiskey at half his usual price.

"I tasted it," Anderson said. "It was green." He refused to buy.

"Penney got hot under the collar. He cussed me out and swore he'd get my ass. Check with my customers who were there that night, they'll tell you. The guy was hollering so loud you could have heard him across the river in Indiana. I kicked him out of the club. I guess this ridiculous murder rap is his attempt to get revenge. Hell, why would I have to pull off a robbery? My club's doing okay. Besides, if I had done it, do you think I'd be sitting here waiting for you coppers? I'd be in South America by now."

Did he own the Buick?

"Yeah, and I reported it stolen over a week ago."

The story checked out.

Where was he on the night of the murders?

"Where I am every Saturday night," Anderson replied. "At my club." He produced witnesses to corroborate the claim.

On the day the Lexington officials delivered Penney from Fort Worth back to Lexington, investigators informed him that his accusation against Bob Anderson leaked like a sieve. It would be his word against Anderson's, and Anderson had a better story.

Penney thought for a moment. "What if there were two witnesses against him?"

Wary, investigators nonetheless agreed that a second witness would probably seal Anderson's fate.

"There *is* a second witness," Penney volunteered. "Raymond Baxter. He helped me plan the caper."

Raymond Baxter was also well known to Lexington authorities. A confessed drug addict, he had been arrested on several occasions. Over the years he had lived hand-to-mouth, shifting from one menial job to another until two years ago, when he found a permanent niche—greenskeeper at the Lexington Country Club. He had been hired by Elsie Miley who, to the consternation of her friends, welcomed the pitiable Baxter like a son.

Arrested within the hour, Baxter confessed to taking part in the crime. Asked if Bob Anderson had been involved, Baxter wavered. Pressed, he finally asked, "What did Tom say?"

"He fingered Anderson," police replied.

"Yeah? Well, sure, Bob was in on it, too."

Cooperative to a fault, Penney led police to Fontaine Ferry Park in Louisville, where, from beneath a shrub he pointed out, they dug up a sack in which Mrs. Miley kept club receipts. In the sack were two pistols, one a .32-caliber, the other a .38. Ballistics tests revealed that the two bullets that killed Marion Miley and the three that killed her mother had all been fired from the same gun—the .32 pistol.

With two witnesses against him, Anderson was indicted along with Penney and Baxter for first-degree murder.

At Anderson's trial, Penney turned state's evidence. He testified that he and Baxter planned the robbery one evening at a night club near Lexington. Baxter had mentioned the large amount of money that Mrs. Miley took in each week at the Lexington Country Club. He said the money was stored downstairs over the weekend in an unguarded cash box. The pickings were too easy to pass up, Penney testified. He offered Baxter a share of the loot if he would simply leave the club house door unlocked one night. Baxter agreed.

The following day, Penney testified, he hitchhiked to Louisville and went to The Cat and Fiddle at 1901 West Main Street. He'd done business with the owner, Bob Anderson, before. He drank a few beers, then mentioned the Lexington caper to Anderson. "It'd be worth ten, maybe fifteen grand."

Anderson was excited about the idea, Penny testified. The nightclub owner demanded to be cut in on the deal. "Next Saturday night I hitchhiked back to Louisville and waited on a side street until Bob picked me up."

Prosecuting Attorney Jim Park, a tall, esteemed Kentucky attorney with a reputation for being scrupulously fair, questioned Penney about the events of that night.

"What time was the pick up?"

"Eleven o'clock," Penney replied.

"In the 1941 Buick?"

"Yes."

They drove to Lexington, Penney continued, where they marked time at a local bar. Shortly after 2:00 A.M. they left the bar and drove out Paris Pike to the Country Club.

"Bob was driving?" Park asked.

"Yes," Penny replied.

As they approached the gates, Penny said, Bob turned off the lights and drove onto the grounds. There were two cars parked in front of the darkened clubhouse. He and Bob discussed the two cars, Penny said, and finally decided that they both belonged to Mrs. Miley.

They parked beside the two cars, tied handkerchiefs to their faces, and pulled on gloves. They went to the door that Baxter had agreed to leave open. It was locked.

The locked door infuriated Anderson, Penny testified. Bob cursed and threatened to "get Baxter" for the oversight. They went around to the side of the building, where Anderson jimmied a basement window, Penny said. He crawled in, then unlocked the kitchen door and let Anderson in. They located the main power switch, turned off all the power, then, working with flashlights, located the clubhouse office and the cash box. The box was empty.

"This time, Bob went into a real rage," Penny said. "He tore that office to shreds trying to find where the old woman had hidden the money."

Unsuccessful, Anderson threw the bolt to the front door, Penney said, ran to the car, and returned with two pistols. He handed one of the guns to Penney, then grabbed an iron counterweight lying loose beneath one of the windows. Anderson rushed up the stairs and Penny followed, knocking over a floor lamp at the head of the landing. When they reached the apartment door, it was locked.

"Bob began beating the door with the iron bar. When it splintered open, there was a woman standing just inside in her nightgown. Bob grabbed her and demanded to know where the money was hidden. Before she could answer . . . he shot her."

Just at that moment, Penney testified, someone grabbed him by the shoulder and spun him around. A fist slammed into his face and he fell to the floor.

Stunned, Penney said he glanced up to see Anderson shoot the unexpected second person, a younger woman, in the back. The young woman took a single step toward Anderson, then collapsed. "Bob reached down and shot her in the top of the head."

The older woman, who had watched her daughter being shot, was still alive. "Bob began to pistol-whip her, demanding money. She pleaded with him to stop. She said all the money she had was in a sack in her dresser."

Anderson kicked the woman back to her bedroom, Penney said, then ransacked the dresser until he found the sack.

"How much money did it contain?" the prosecutor asked.

"A hundred and forty dollars," Penney replied.

They tore the place apart, Penney said, but didn't find another cent.

The older woman had collapsed and didn't seem to be breathing. Convinced that both women were dead, Penney testified, he and Anderson fled the clubhouse.

"Bob ordered me to drive. When we got to the gate we spotted another car pulling out of the club driveway just ahead of us. Bob began to cuss. He was afraid the driver might have spotted the Buick. We drove back to Louisville and buried the sack and the guns in the park. Then Bob gave me some money and told me to high-tail it out of the state with the car."

"Where did you go?" the prosecutor asked.

"Florida," Penney replied. Then, after a couple of days, he headed for Texas. He didn't know that the day he left Louisville, Anderson reported his car stolen.

On October 9 Penney was captured in Fort Worth.

It was damning testimony and the prosecuting attorney was determined to set the most damaging points in the juror's minds.

He asked, "Once again, who was armed with the thirty-two pistol?"

"Anderson," Penney replied.

"He shot the two women?"

"Yes."

"Why did he begin shooting?"

"To keep the old woman from screaming."

The prosecution rested.

Unlike Penney and Baxter, whose indigence compelled them to trust their fates to court-appointed attorneys, Anderson hired one of the most prestigious legal firms in Louisville. To discredit the state's star witness, Anderson's attorneys laid Penney's sordid history of arrests, convictions, and tainted prison record before the jury. Then they turned to a specific attack on his testimony.

Defense: Why did you say in Fort Worth that Anderson was your only accomplice, then once back in Lexington change your story and say that Baxter was your accomplice?

Penney: Baxter *was* an accomplice.

Defense: Isn't it true that Baxter was your only accomplice?

Penney: No. Baxter wasn't even in the clubhouse. Anderson was with me.

Defense: Did you make a deal with the prosecution?

Penney: No.

Defense: Isn't it true that you agreed to testify against Anderson in exchange for a life sentence?

Penney: No.

Defense: Do you hope for a life sentence?

Penney: No, no hope. Most likely I'll burn.

Taken aback by this response, the defense changed the line of questioning.

Defense: Isn't it true that on September twenty-third, five days before the murders, you had a heated argument with Bob Anderson over a business deal?

Penney: Yes.

Defense: And you swore to get even.

Penney: Yes.

Defense: And naming him as your accomplice in this crime is your way of getting even, isn't it?

Penney: No. He *was* my accomplice.

Defense: Isn't it true that on the night before the crime you went to Mister Anderson's place of business and stole his car to use in the crime?

Penney: No, it's not true.

Throughout the cross-examination, Penney stuck to his story. Then Baxter took the stand and corroborated Penney's testimony in detail.

On re-direct, Prosecutor Park suggested that by reporting his Buick stolen, Anderson was using a ploy to cover up the fact of its disappearance. As for the witnesses who saw Anderson in The Cat and Fiddle on the night of the murders, the latest sighting was at 10:30 P.M., leaving ample time for him to have met Penney at 11:00 P.M. as Penney testified.

Unlike the juries for Penney and Baxter, who reached guilty verdicts in minutes, Anderson's jury deliberated for twenty-four hours. At last, persuaded by Penney's testimony and Baxter's corroboration, they returned a verdict of guilty.

Sentenced to die in the electric chair, the three men were transferred to the state penitentiary in Eddyville.

Anderson's conviction was not hailed universally. News accounts reported a widespread feeling that the trial revealed a conspiracy to convict Anderson regardless of the law and the evidence. Nonetheless, the Court of Appeals upheld the sentences. The executions were scheduled for shortly after midnight, New Year's Day, 1943.

Around the country and in Europe, Marion Miley's friends

and mourners were satisfied. In Lexington, the police blotter was closed on the case.

Then, a bizarre turn of events transformed the cut-and-dried case into a cause célèbre.

During the year immediately following his capture, Tom Penney underwent an extraordinary transformation. At the urging of two nuns who visited him in the Lexington jail before and during the trials, he began to study Scripture. Previously contemptuous of religion, totally devoid of a spiritual nature, he was nonetheless a voracious reader. During every spare moment, he pored over material the nuns supplied him. At last, to the skepticism of those who knew him best, he requested formal instruction in Catholicism.

No man could have been better suited to the priestly task he was about to undertake than Father George Donnelly. Tall, eloquent, with an air of no-nonsense authority, Father Donnelly was nonetheless a patient and understanding tutor. From the outset, Tom Penney recognized that he could place full trust in the fair-complexioned curate with the silky white hair. In January 1942 the priest and the convict began to spend long hours together in Penney's cell. Some prominent members of the Church hierarchy frowned on Father Donnelly's dedication of so much time to the convicted killer and told him so. Unintimidated, the priest persevered. Over the course of the next twelve months, first in Lexington and continuing in Eddyville, he methodically guided Tom Penney to what Catholic historians would later chronicle as one of the most dramatic acts of repentance and reversals of character in modern Church history.

And it was in the bloom of his new-found faith that Penney dropped the bombshell that turned the Miley case topsy-turvy. Two weeks before the scheduled executions, Penney requested a private meeting with Warden Buchanan. That afternoon in the warden's office, Penney said, "I lied about Bob. He wasn't in on the murders. I stole his car like he said. He messed me up over a liquor deal and I wanted to get even. I'm sorry and want to make amends."

His testimony at the trial had otherwise been true, Penney

claimed, except for the name of his accomplice.

"Who was the accomplice?" Buchanan asked.

"Buford Stewart," Penney replied. "We were pals. We pulled off a couple of hijackings together before the Miley caper."

A small-time Louisville bartender, Buford Stewart had a police record for a series of minor offenses.

The warden dismissed Penney and had Raymond Baxter brought to his office. "Willie," the warden said, "Tom says he lied about Bob Anderson. He says he wasn't your accomplice in the murders."

"Who'd he say was?" Baxter asked.

"You tell me," Buchanan countered.

The little man gave a wry grin. "Did he say . . . Buford Stewart?"

Warden Buchanan called Anderson's attorneys at once. Next morning at the prison, in the attorneys' presence, Penney and Baxter repeated their new version of the crime. That afternoon, Penney penned a deposition by hand that matched his court testimony in nearly every detail except one—Buford Stewart's name replaced Bob Anderson's.

Once again the Miley case became the hottest crime story in Kentucky and beyond. Editorial sentiments ranged from "I told you so" to disdain of the new story, and with reason. Buford Stewart could not defend himself. On February 2, 1942, four months after the Miley murders, the thirty-four-year-old bartender had been killed in a street brawl in Louisville.

Anderson petitioned for a stay of execution. The state's attorney advised caution. Naming a dead man as an alibi was a timeworn trick.

But the alibi had not come from Bob Anderson, the beneficiary. It had been volunteered by Tom Penney, who had nothing to gain other than, as he claimed, "a clear conscience." Impressed with Penney's sincerity, the Court of Appeals granted Anderson a stay, with the stipulation that he file at once for a new trial.

The ruling put the state in a quandary. If Penney and Baxter were executed as scheduled, the state would lose its only witnesses—albeit recanting witnesses now—against Anderson. With no alternative, the state petitioned for and won a stay of execution for Penney and Baxter.

It was a brand new ball game.

Then, as abruptly as he had rekindled the issue, the increasingly mercurial Penney dropped another bombshell. Two weeks after exonerating Anderson, Penney requested a news conference. To reporters assembled before his death-house cell he said, "I have made my peace with God. My conscience is clear."

Then, in a ringing declaration, he announced: "From this moment on I will say no more about the Miley case, ever."

Anderson and his attorneys were stunned. Surely Penney's new stance didn't mean that he would refuse to testify at Anderson's upcoming hearing for a new trial?

Indeed, it did, Penny proclaimed.

Nonetheless, Anderson's petition had been granted and the hearing had been scheduled.

On January 24, 1943, Warden Buchanan, accompanied by prison officials and state police, delivered Anderson, Penney, and Baxter to Lexington, where the convicted trio appeared before the Fayette County Court considering Anderson's petition for a new trial. True to his word, Penney stood mute throughout the hearing, refusing to discuss the case or explain his silence. Defense attorneys were perplexed. Anderson was enraged.

In light of Penney's lack of corroboration, the court refused to accept his handwritten deposition exonerating Anderson. With no new evidence to consider, Anderson's appeal for a new trial was denied. The execution date for all three men was rescheduled for early Friday morning, February 26.

"Tonight," Tom Waller uttered to himself as he closed the MILEY CASE file and placed it back in his HOLD basket.

The veteran attorney sat back in his seat, reflecting once again on the material he had just re-read. Which of Penney's conflicting stories about Anderson was true? It was no secret in the legal profession that many lawyers, including some in his own firm, doubted Penney's original testimony indicting the Louisville tavern owner. It was simply too pat, too seemingly contrived for vengeance, coming as it did so soon on the heels of Penney's ringing declaration to "get even" with the Louisville nightclub owner. The doubters were relieved when Penney refuted his original accusation against Anderson, then dumbfounded when he turned mute.

And Baxter? Waller mused. That insignificant, puppet-like little man. Who could rely on anything he said? Was he even mentally competent? Though an admitted accomplice in the robbery, he had forgotten his one simple chore—to leave a door unlocked. Had he truly committed a capital offense?

What a quandary. Surely the case hinged on something yet unknown, something most probably locked away forever in Tom Penney's brain.

Forever?

Perhaps not. There was an important figure in what remained of the Marion Miley murder case—Warden Jesse Buchanan. Waller thought back to the day Buchanan came to see him in torment over the prospect of executing an innocent man. Doggedly persistent, as always, the warden was searching for the truth that day, and he would undoubtedly search for the truth until the last moment.

After all was said and done, Waller reflected, if anyone could solve the riddle of Tom Penney, Jess Buchanan was the man to do it.

4

William Jesse Buchanan was born in an era and locality where children were expected to contribute to their family's welfare and were often beget with that purpose in mind. The fifth of seven siblings—four boys, three girls—he was assigned chores on the family's hard-scrabble Union County farm before he was old enough to attend school. By age six, he was responsible to help hoe the garden, gather coal and kindling for the cooking range, clean the chicken house, and gather eggs. By age ten, he could hook up the family mule and "plow a straight furrow" from sunup to sundown, then wrestle or play rough-tag with his brothers half the night before crawling into the straw-mattress bed he shared with two of them. At age twelve, he was tutored by his father in the hallowed Scottish trade of stone masonry. By age fifteen, he had perfected that talent to where he was much in demand by land owners needing cisterns lined, chimneys built, and pasture walls erected.

Always what was termed in those days "a hoss," he was the strongest of four powerful brothers, a fact they learned each in his own time, the hard way. Beginning in his teen years, his legendary strength became a crucial family asset. His older brother, James, also a giant of a man, had suffered a brain injury at birth. Predisposed to violent seizures that could strike at any time, he would lash out at anything and anybody in his path, once badly injuring his elder sister Nolie with a blow to her face. One evening at supper, when James was twenty-two, he emitted an anguished cry, jumped to his feet, and started beating the table with both fists. Seated next to him, eighteen-year-old Jess stood, locked his brother in a bear hug, and held on. For five minutes, the enraged James fought in vain to break the steel-trap grip. Jess continued the rigid embrace until his brother collapsed into the deep sleep that often followed his seizures. Thereafter, whenever Jess was nearby when James was stricken, the younger brother would bear-hug his older brother until the spell passed. He was the only person with the necessary brawn to overcome James's frenzied strength. It was a doleful ritual that lasted until James died peacefully in his sleep at age forty-two.

Although he feared no man, Buchanan was afraid of the dark. Once, at a carnival in Morganfield where he consumed too many beers, his friends locked him in a nearby horse barn to sleep it off. He awakened to the pitch darkness of a tiny stall. Not knowing where he was, he became frantic and crawled along the dirt floor until he came up against a wooden wall. Jumping to his feet, he began to kick the wall with all his strength. In minutes, the entire side of the barn collapsed outward, bringing the rest of the building down around his head. In view of startled spectators, he walked out into the carnival brightness, uninjured. For the next three weeks, under his persuasive supervision, his friends rebuilt the structure.

Once asked why he feared the darkness, he attributed it to an older sister who teased him from the time he was a toddler about "goblins" that were coming to get him as soon as the lights went out. Often during those boyhood years, he would lie awake all night, terrified. When he was old enough to do so, he demanded that a lamp be kept burning throughout the night where he could see it from his bed. In later years the lamp became an electric light, and it remained an uncompromising requirement for the rest of his life.

As his reputation grew, friends began to encourage Jess Buchanan to run for public office. Sheriff was the position most often mentioned. To test the waters, he accepted a commission as Deputy Sheriff from Judge A. W. Clements. His fellow deputy was Earle Clements, later to become U.S. Senator from Kentucky. Recalling their tenure together, Earl Clements would remark: "Jess Buchanan is the only man I ever met who could quell a riot just by stepping into the room."

In 1925 Buchanan married Clements's divorced sister-in-law, Margaret Kagy Clements, from Uniontown, taking her two children to raise as his own. Over the years, two more children were born to the union. About his wife, Buchanan often remarked that the wisest move he ever made in life was to "marry above myself."

Discovering a passion for law enforcement, in the same summer he got married, Buchanan followed the advice of his constituents and entered the race for sheriff. He won handily.

That was the job he held the following year, when the infamous Birger gang decided to invade Union County. In the rich annals of the Ohio River Valley of Western Kentucky, no story is more revered than that of the time the notorious Birger gang came up against Big Jess Buchanan.

Charley Birger was one of the most notorious outlaws in the Midwest. Rivaling Capone, whose murderous tactics he admired, Birger masterminded a widespread gambling and bootleg-whiskey operation from a well-guarded headquarters in Central Illinois. In the winter of 1926 he decided to expand operation into Kentucky, just across the river.

On Christmas Eve three of Birger's lieutenants crossed the Ohio on the Shawneetown Ferry in their Oldsmobile touring car to scout the territory. That afternoon, in the rural village of Henshaw, they were caught in a severe snowstorm. Roads became impassable. To occupy their time the three decided to raise a little hell. Throughout that afternoon and night, fortified by their stock-in-trade, 100-proof moonshine bourbon, they terrorized the three hundred peaceable citizens of Henshaw by taking pot-shots at road signs, store windows, and stray dogs and cats.

Late Christmas morning, while frightened residents remained barricaded in their homes, Reverend H. B. Self, pastor of the Henshaw Christian Church, succeeded in getting a telephone call through to Sheriff Jess Buchanan in Morganfield, ten miles away.

Buchanan pondered the complaint. The roads to Henshaw were impassable, but there was a solution.

"Brother Self," Buchanan said, "those fellows aren't going anywhere in this storm. I'll be down on the four o'clock train to arrest them. You tell them that."

Braving the elements, Reverend Self found two of the trio, haggard from a night of carousing, seated at a back table in Gilbert Vaughn's general store. At the meat counter, Vaughn was reluctantly preparing two baloney sandwiches. The third culprit was nowhere in sight.

Reverend Self delivered Sheriff Buchanan's message.

The two men stared at the preacher in disbelief, then doubled over in laughter. "Arrest us! You hear that, Ed," one of the men said. "Some hayseed sheriff's comin' down here on the train to run us in. God, is that rich!" He guffawed again. "Hey, when's the last time you plugged a badge?"

The man called Ed wiped tears of laughter from his eyes. "No need to waste lead." He withdrew a four-inch Russell Barlow switch-blade knife from his pocket and flipped it open. Spitting in his hand, he began to hone the blade against his palm. "Gawdamighty, Hank . . . this trip might turn out to be worthwhile after all."

Throughout the afternoon, between eating and swilling booze, the two men described to the preacher and the storekeeper

34

the gruesome reception they planned for the sheriff.

At 4:40, a distant whistle signaled the arrival of the inbound train. The man called Hank perked up. "Hey, Ed, let's take the hayseed's nose back to Charley."

Fingering his knife, Ed heartily endorsed the idea. "Maybe Charley will give us a bonus," he said, and they both settled back to wait.

Minutes later the front door opened and a gust of frigid air swept through the store. Crowding the doorway from hinge to latch, a giant man stooped low to clear the lintel and entered the room. The newcomer was wearing whipcord trousers with legs stuffed in the tops of size-15 lace-up boots. His heavy plaid Mackinaw coat, to which was pinned a six-pointed star, was buttoned snugly around his 22-inch neck. His broad-brimmed gray felt hat would have served any lesser man as an umbrella. The mackinaw was drawn back on the right side to reveal a holstered, silver-plated, stag-handle Smith and Wesson .44 Special revolver that looked every bit as formidable as the man wearing it.

The two scofflaws sat transfixed as Sheriff Buchanan stomped snow from his boots and walked over to them. He laid a ham-sized hand in front of Ed and tapped the table. "Put that knife down right here, son. If you boys got guns, lay them out here too . . . *now*."

Two snub-nose .38s immediately appeared on the table.

The sheriff grasped each man by the shoulder, welding them to their seats. "Where's your friend?"

"Down . . . down by the depot," Ed said. He mentioned the name of a woman who lived in a shanty at the edge of town.

Buchanan picked up the knife and the pistols and put them in his coat pocket. "You boys just sit right here. I'm going to get your friend, then we're all going to catch the evening train back to Morganfield."

The sheriff turned and strode out the door without looking back.

Ed and Hank looked at each other sheepishly. At the counter, Reverend Self and Storekeeper Vaughn were grinning ear to ear.

After a long while, Hank said, "Ed, I thought you were going to cut him up."

"Oh, sure," Ed retorted, "and I thought you were gonna take his nose back to Charley."

The two looked at each other for a moment. Then, with a resolute shake of his head, Hank exclaimed, "Ed, I'd rather climb a thorn tree naked with a bobcat under each armpit than rile that big son of a bitch!"

The story is not apocryphal. It happened. And it became part of the legend.

One who heard it was Governor Ruby LaFoon.

LaFoon came into office during hard times. A relentless depression gripped the land. Across the nation, desperate men tramped the roadways by day and huddled around hobo fires by night, fruitlessly searching for livelihood in an era gone haywire. Committed to change, LaFoon was contemplating remedies not popular with the political Old Guard who saw their privileged status threatened. He wanted a man of courage in his office as a buffer between himself and the power brokers. He sent for Jess Buchanan.

Buchanan arrived in Frankfort on an unseasonably warm but cloudy day. As he left the train station to hail a taxi he passed a clothing store that catered to large men. On display in the window was a single-breasted seersucker jacket, size 58 Extra Long, special sale price, $6.50. Buchanan looked woefully at his frayed blue-serge coat. He took out his wallet and counted his money. He had his return ticket and enough money for supper, but if he bought the seersucker jacket he wouldn't be able to afford to take a taxi to the Capitol, a mile and a half up the hill on the other side of the Kentucky River. Still, for an interview with the governor. . . .

He relented and entered the store.

Fifteen minutes later he emerged proudly wearing his first new coat in six years and began the long walk up Capital Avenue.

He had gone about a half-mile when he felt the first raindrops. A minute later he was caught in a blinding downpour, and he still had a mile to go.

Governor LaFoon was at his desk that day when his secretary stepped into his office. "Governor"—she barely suppressed a giggle—"you *must* see this."

LaFoon, who never tired of telling the story, described the sight: "There were a dozen or so legislators and lobbyists waiting in the lounge. In their midst, towering above all, stood Jess Buchanan. He was drenched to his skin, his hat had collapsed down around his ears, and he was standing in a ever widening puddle of water. He was wearing a seersucker coat that had shriveled up about ten sizes too small for him. It lacked about a foot of closing across his belly. The bottom had shrunk up to his belt, the sleeves had shriveled at least six inches up his wrists. It was truly a comical sight. But you know what? No one of those hard-nosed jackals out there was laughing. I hired Jess on the spot."

He stayed with LaFoon for two years, then in 1934 he was appointed Deputy U.S. Marshal for Western Kentucky, where his reputation as a lawman spread. In 1935, U.S. Attorney General Homer Cummings offered Buchanan a promotion and his pick of districts west of the Mississippi River. Buchanan declined on the grounds that he could not leave his native state.

In 1936, newly elected Governor A. B. "Happy" Chandler, faced with growing unrest over primitive penal conditions, called Buchanan to Frankfort and asked him to take over the job of warden of the Kentucky State Penitentiary at Eddyville.

Buchanan had known Chandler since the governor was a youngster. He liked and admired him. Still, he demurred.

Sensing the reason, the young governor said, "I understand your reluctance, Jess. Our penitentiaries have been run like Banana Republics. No one knows who's in charge. Hell, Ruby LaFoon had to promise those convicts down there ham and eggs for breakfast to keep them from taking over the joint. Well, I not going to give in to that sort of blackmail. If you take the job at Eddyville, *you* will be in charge. I'll back you all the way."

It was a persuasive proposal. Buchanan accepted.

◆　◆　◆

Kentucky's maximum security prison sat high atop a bluff overlooking the Cumberland River in the small town of Eddyville in the western extremity of the Bluegrass state. In June 1936, one month after his fifty-third birthday, Jess Buchanan arrived to take charge at the institution. He was not prepared for what he found.

Conditions at the prison were shocking. The fortress-like "Castle on the Cumberland" housed the dregs of the state's criminal element. Among an inmate population of 1,262 (jammed into facilities built for 800) were murderers, rapists, armed robbers, child molesters, kidnappers, gang lords, recidivists, and other assorted thugs. Mixed indiscriminately with this hardcore element, often sharing the same cell, were youthful first-termers incarcerated for minor offenses.

Sanitary conditions were deplorable. Litter and debris cluttered the prison yard and the four cellblocks. In the kitchen and dining hall, where summer temperatures sometimes reached 130 degrees, the stoves, cooking utensils, floors, and eating tables were caked with filth. One cook's sole duty was to fish cockroaches out of the food before it was delivered from the kitchen to the dining room.

The bare-subsistence diet, 1,000 calories per man per day, was mostly carbohydrates. Rampant among the inmate population were diseases of the skin, eyes, lips, membranes, mouth, throat, and bones.

Unaffected by these irritants were the "Moguls." Living in relative splendor in well-furnished cells on the top tier of Cellblock Four, a score of pampered convicts slept on innerspring mattresses, came and went within the confines of the prison as they pleased, ate food delivered from the outside, and, in some cases, had convict servants to attend to their needs. Politically or financially powerful, or having feared underworld connections, the Moguls received deferential treatment from inmates and guards alike.

Among the staff, all of them political appointees, was a small core of professionals dedicated to proper prison operations. All they needed was leadership. Within seventy-two hours of his arrival, Warden Buchanan had identified every man in this category.

One was Porter Lady.

Painstakingly efficient in his job as Cellblock Supervisor, articulate and a natty dresser, thirty-six-year-old Porter Lady was regarded by his colleagues as a dandy. For the first week, Lady's relationship with the new warden was discreetly proper. Then, late one night, Lady came to the prison and asked to speak to the warden in private.

"If I've misjudged you," Lady said to Buchanan that evening, "I'm putting my job on the line. But there's something I think you should see."

They went to Cellblock One. In a remote corner of the basement Lady lifted a manhole cover and shined his flashlight down a flight of stone steps. The steps led to a narrow tunnel that opened onto a cavernous room. At the far end of the clammy chamber, Lady shined the light onto two dungeon cells. Buchanan stared incredulously. At the front of one cell a man stood hand-cuffed to the bars with his feet barely touching the floor. Bearded and soiled by his own wastes, he looked more animal than human. The shackled man moaned and closed his eyes to avoid the painful light.

Buchanan seethed. "How long has he been here?"

"Thirty days."

Thirty days suspended in a dank dungeon totally devoid of light. Let down for fifteen minutes each midnight to relieve himself in a slop bucket, gobble down a single daily meal with his bare hands, then strung up again. Watered twice a day by a convict who held a dipper to his lips.

Lady said, "His infraction was—"

"I don't give a damn what his infraction was," Buchanan said, his voice cold with fury. "I want that man taken to the infirmary at once. If you don't have the keys, cut those damned bars down." He took a couple of breaths to bring his anger under control. "And Porter . . . thank you."

One week later, Buchanan received a letter from Governor Chandler listing the names of nine guards and other officials at the institution whom the governor wanted dismissed at once. The first name on the list was Porter Lady. It was followed by the names of Sam Litchfield, Clyde Twisdale, Tom Woodward, and five others that Buchanan had determined to be first-rate men.

Buchanan felt betrayed. He had been promised autonomy. Now the young Governor he had trusted and forfeited a secure federal appointment to serve was defaulting on his word.

That night, alone at his desk, Buchanan penned his resignation as warden. At 3:00 A.M. the next morning, he left Eddyville for a four-hour drive to Frankfort. When Governor Chandler arrived at his office in the Capitol that day, Buchanan was waiting.

The governor studied the list of names over his signature. "Jess, I never saw this letter before in my life."

The letter, typed on Chandler's official stationary, was a clever forgery.

"Jess," the governor said, "I don't care how many orders you get to fire or hire people, you make the decision as you see fit. If you think a person is necessary for the competent operation of that institution, you keep him—even if the order to fire him comes from me."

Reassured of Chandler's integrity, Buchanan departed for Eddyville without ever showing the governor his handwritten resignation.

Subsequent investigation into the bogus letter from Governor Chandler established that a prominent state legislator filched the stationery from the governor's office, brought it to Eddyville, where a Lyon County executive typed the firing order and forged Chandler's signature, and carried it back to Frankfort to mail so that it would bear the capital city postmark. Such was the state of prison politics.

The day after returning from Frankfort, Buchanan announced the immediate dismissal of eleven officers and guards from the prison staff. Then he announced that he was establishing a new position at the prison, Chief of Staff, accountable only to the warden and responsible to assure that the warden's policies were implemented without question. The new

Chief of Staff—Porter Lady.

With his promotion, Lady received his first orders.

"To begin with," Buchanan said, "I want that dungeon sealed off. Fill the damned thing with cement. I never want it usable again.

"Next, I want this institution cleaned up, top to bottom. Put mop and bucket crews on it and keep them on it every day until I tell you I'm satisfied. From now on it will be the guard captains' responsibility to see that the yards and cells stay clean, and I'm going to inspect them myself every day.

"Next, I'm disbanding the Disciplinary Committee. There'll be no committees making decisions here while I'm warden.

"Next, I want new cellblock assignments—maximum to minimum. I'll decide with your help who goes where. I don't care how much shuffling it takes or who screams; I want young boys and first offenders kept away from the heavyweights.

"Finally, tell the kitchen supervisor that any cockroaches I find in the food from now on, he's going to eat."

Lady could hardly suppress his enthusiasm. "Yes sir!"

"And Porter . . . one more thing. Put those damned Moguls on the scrub brushes."

No coddler of convicts, Warden Buchanan nonetheless demanded that they be treated humanely. In following weeks, he focused on upgrading the inmate diet. On advice from a physician, the first addition to the menu was citric acid. Every second day, lemonade was served with the evening meal. As they could be afforded, fresh fruits and vegetables were added. Then, an unheard of luxury: meat once a week. Slowly, inmate health problems began to wane.

Staff positions were restructured. Rejecting the commonly held view at many state prisons that any man who could turn a key and shoot a gun was qualified to be a prison guard, Buchanan instituted a classification system for employees. Guards who were excellent marksmen but poor in one-to-one situations with inmates were assigned to wall-tower duty. Others who couldn't hit the broadside of a barn at ten paces but were cool in trying circumstances were assigned to yard and cellblock duty. Every man was used where his talents best served the institution.

It was the beginning of one of the most esteemed prison administrations in American history. Over the next two decades, out-of-state wardens, legislative committees, officials from the American Prison Congress, and a Chief Justice of the United States would visit Eddyville to study Warden Buchanan's innovative, hands-on methods.

It was all accomplished by a man whose formal education ended with the sixth grade.

5

Sooner or later, all new wardens are tested. The test for Warden Buchanan and the innovative changes he brought about at Eddyville came on Saturday, August 7, 1937—a day he was absent from the institution.

It had been planned that way.

Just inside the prison yard to the rear of the administration building was a timeworn two-story red brick building as old as the institution. It was the inmate kitchen and dining hall. The upper floor of the old building contained twenty-four rows of long wooden tables with side benches where the inmates ate their meals. The first floor contained the kitchen and bakery, where a score of cooks toiled over eight massive coal-burning ranges preparing three meals each day for 1,230 men. Food from the kitchen was hoisted to the upper-floor dining room on a manually operated dumbwaiter and set on tables where each man's army-type mess tray was served cafeteria style by cook's helpers.

On Friday evening, the day before, three men were involved in a clandestine operation in the bakery storeroom in the basement of the kitchen. Laboriously, they hoisted fifty-pound sacks of flour and moved them from one side of the storeroom to the other. After a while one of the younger men stopped. "Damn it, Bob, my back's killing me. Are you sure you got the right dope about this?"

"Keep working, Earl," Robert McNair replied. "I'm sure."

A handsome, square-jawed man of muscular build, thirty-seven-year-old Bob McNair exuded an air of arrogant self-confidence. Among the convict population he was regarded as a person one should defer to, or avoid.

Earl Gibbs, twenty-seven, hoisted another sack. "I don't know. I just don't get it how all of a sudden you figure that tomorrow's the right day."

The third man, twenty-three-year-old Ezra Dehart, spoke up. "Know your problem, Earl? You're yellow."

Gibbs threw to the floor the heavy sack he'd just hoisted. "Dammit, Dehart! I'm not taking anymore lip from a scum-sucking punk like you." He made a threatening move toward Gibbs, who didn't cower.

McNair stepped between the two younger men. "Cut it out! Now!"

Neither of the adversaries doubted the husky McNair's ability to enforce the order. Gibbs lowered his fist.

"That's better" McNair said. "Now listen good, both of you. Tomorrow *is* the right day. I'll explain it later. Right now, keep cracking on those sacks."

The two men gave each other contemptuous looks, then returned to their tasks.

Five minutes later, Dehart cried out: "Hey, Bob! C'mere!"

McNair and Gibbs hurried to where Dehart stood pointing to a flour sack. It looked identical to the others, with a minute exception: the top seal was sewn with pale yellow, rather than white, thread.

McNair lifted the sack to a nearby table and slit it down the middle with his bakers knife. He plunged his hands into the flour and groped about. After a moment he broke into a wide grin. He withdrew a small bundle from the sack and laid it on the table with care, as if he were handling fine crystal. Removing the oilcloth wrapping, he lifted a snub-nose .38-caliber Colt revolver.

"Jesus," Dehart exclaimed. "Look at that baby!"

McNair checked the cylinder. The pistol was loaded. He rewrapped the gun in the oilcloth, placed it on the bottom of a deep pan, and covered it with flour.

"Know what I hope?" Dehart said. "I hope Buchanan's in the admin building tomorrow when we bust through. I'd love to put one of those lead slugs through his gut."

McNair gave a mirthless laugh. "You got the brains of a jackass, Ezra. If you'd read anything in the papers except the comics you'd know Buchanan's going to be in Owensboro tomorrow, making a speech to a bunch of Feds. That's why I decided tomorrow's our day. We don't want him anywhere near this place when we break through. Trust me. I know him a hell of a lot better than either one of you do. He's one bad-ass son of a bitch!"

He let the point sink in, then ordered the two back up to the bakery. "I've still got things to do down here."

Dehart and Gibbs returned to the bakery to finish their shift. McNair remained behind to think things through yet again.

Robert McNair had good reason for his assessment of Jesse Buchanan. He had locked horns with him once, long before the new warden came to Eddyville.

A Jack-of-all-crimes, McNair's most lucrative enterprise in those years was running "moon" out of Eastern Kentucky. Down Thunder Road to Knoxville and Nashville, and up Nightmare Alley to Cincinnati. He had a reputation for being the best in the business. He drove a souped-up Ford V-8 with a false rear seat and a sealed trunk that hid two frame-mounted stainless steel tanks. In an emergency, even with a full load, he could peg the needle at 100. But he was careful to obey the speed laws, town and rural, so as not to draw unwarranted attention from the local law. Still, it wasn't the village constables or hick sheriffs that worried him. Most of them had their palms out, and a couple hundred dollars now and then guaranteed most county roads would be safe.

It was the Feds who were the problem. It took steel nerves and a sixth sense to stay ahead of the despised revenuers—the U.S. Marshals. McNair prided himself there, too. Possessing a legendary sixth sense, he could smell a road block a mile away, and more than once he had ripped a new road through a field of corn in a hasty change of itinerary.

He was also proud of his product. He hauled good stuff: hundred-proof bourbon, brewed in remote Cumberland hideaways by master distillers who drip-cured each drop through charcoal until it took on the hue of rich amber. Smooth, easy-sipping whiskey, it was a far cry from the quick-cured, lye-treated "white lightning" being produced by disreputable shiners over in Harlan and Breathit Counties and shipped east to Atlantic City and New York. A single pint of that searing rot-gut could blind or kill a person. No, McNair's cargo was always first-rate, his take was top dollar, and he was thinking about expanding. Getting a couple of more Fords, maybe. Training his own drivers.

Then came the night of Frog Island.

With the repeal of the Volstead Act, which had enforced prohibition throughout the land, alcoholic beverages were once again legal. The lucrative eastern markets, which once depended on the moonshiners, turned to legitimate sources. To compete with the legal booze, bootleggers were forced to change tactics. One was to drastically lower their prices. Another was to expand into new markets.

One August evening, McNair received a call from a broker in Paducah. The markets in St. Louis and Little Rock were ripe for good moon, the man claimed. He needed premium bourbon fast and was offering a $300 bonus over the going rate.

McNair had never dealt with the broker, but a grapevine check of his credentials revealed him to be an ex-con, a rum-runner himself in earlier years, and more recently a distributor for Capone. No reference could bear more credence. The first delivery was set for a Monday, two weeks hence.

His best source for good bourbon was in Letcher County, 375 miles from Paducah. McNair made the wholesale purchase that Monday morning, then waited till noon to depart, scheduling himself for a slow run to arrive after dark. For the first five hours the leisurely trip through the rolling bluegrass hills of central Kentucky was uneventful. McNair swigged black coffee from a thermos, ate a couple of baloney sandwiches, stopped once for gas, and mentally catalogued landmarks for future reference. Just past the town of Beaver Dam, Route 62 entered upon a straight, three-mile stretch of blacktop leading to the Green River crossing. Near sundown, McNair rounded the final curve leading to the straightaway. He slowed. Three-quarters of a mile ahead a farm truck lay overturned, blocking one lane of traffic. Some motorists had pulled to the side and were milling around the wreck. A flagman was stopping vehicles, then allowing them to proceed, one by one.

McNair took his place in the line of cars inching toward the flagman. On the ground near the truck, two men lay swathed in bandages. The hairs on McNair's neck pricked up. Something was out of place. The car ahead of him cleared the flagman and drove on. McNair pulled forward and stopped. Then it hit him: bandages, splints—and there wasn't a medic or ambulance in sight. He studied the scene more closely. There were no women or children among the onlookers, nor were there any in the parked cars. Wary, he pushed the clutch to the floor, shifted into first gear, and waited.

The flagman stooped at the window. "May I see your drivers license, please?"

Drivers license? Why the hell would a flagman at an accident be checking drivers licenses? It was a set-up. And he'd driven right into it.

McNair smiled. "Sure."

He made a gesture of reaching into his rear pocket. Then, floor-boarding the accelerator, he released the clutch. Screeching tires welded asphalt and rubber in a flume of white-hot smoke. The Ford shot forward, barely missing men who dived for the ditches. McNair was a hundred yards away before the first shots came. They were followed by a fusillade.

In the mirror he saw men running toward parked cars. He wasn't worried. They wouldn't stand a chance against the souped-up Ford. He pulled a lever on the dash, opening a valve in the secreted cargo tank, and a steady stream of bourbon began to pour out on the highway behind him. Lighter car, more speed. Then he remembered Green River crossing was less than two miles ahead. Damn! It was a ferry crossing, a natural barrier, another trap. Surely the cops had covered that angle. They'd be waiting for him at the river.

He studied the topography on each side of the highway, envisioning the map he'd memorized, as he always did before making a run. According to the map, there was a county road not far ahead that paralleled the river, then backtracked to Beaver Dam. He could outrun his pursuers on that road, hide until nightfall, then double back to the highway and hightail it back to Fletcher County.

The rural turn-off appeared on his right. He wheeled into a sharp dog-leg turn and raced northward over a rutted dirt road that served the scattered farms along the bottom lands. Even here the Ford, with its reinforced frame, springs, and shocks, would have the advantage. Despite his predicament, he felt exhilarated. He'd been in precarious situations before. Indeed, he had a reputation for relishing danger. He thought ahead to the debt he intended to collect in coming weeks—a debt of blood owed by the stoolie broker in Paducah who had help set up this caper.

At that moment the Ford's engine coughed, sputtered, and died.

McNair stared at the gas gauge. Empty! A bullet must have hit the tank. He struck the steering wheel with his fist and began to curse. Then, sucking in a deep breath, he forced himself to think. Rage would not serve him now. He was vulnerable.

A mile behind, a thick cloud of dust marked the oncoming pursuers. Hastily he studied the terrain. There was an endless tobacco field on his right. Too risky for a hiding place. On his left, a quarter-mile downhill, was the river. He grabbed his pistol from beneath the seat, jumped from the car, and ran down the steep embankment. He reached the water just as two cars slid to a stop behind the abandoned Ford. Four men got out and looked around in all directions. McNair wondered if they were local law or the Feds. Then he spotted the man that towered above the others. McNair knew who the giant was. Among those in McNair's trade, the big man had a chilling reputation. He was U.S. Deputy Marshal Jesse Buchanan.

McNair took stock. In another half-hour it would be dark. A hundred yards downstream a narrow backwater slough veered away from the main river and meandered for miles through the woods. The narrow peninsula that lay between the slough and the river was known among locals as Frog Island.

Remote and uninhabited, Frog Island was a trackless wilderness. On the forest floor, sheltered by a broad canopy of oak, black gum, beech, hickory, walnut, and maple trees, fallen timbers lay in various stages of decomposition. This moldering jungle was an Eden for wild animals, reptiles, and insects that thrived on its rich flora, and on each other. For one with knowledge of forests, it was a haven where one could survive indefinitely.

McNair knew forests.

Up on the road the four marshals were huddled. With luck, McNair figured, he could slip down the bank to the slough, wade across, and disappear into the depths of Frog Island without being spotted. Even if he were seen, none of his pursuers would be so foolhardy as to follow him into that jungle. Once in the woods, he would await darkness, then sneak back to Beaver Dam. Hitchhiking was out of the question. By nightfall, every motorist in West Kentucky would have been alerted about him. But on foot, even if he stuck to the back roads and fields, he should be able to reach town in three hours at most. He would steal a car and be back in Letcher Country by dawn.

Crouching low, he ran to the slough and waded in. The waist-deep water was stagnant. A thick blanket of putrid algae covering the surface almost made him gag. But with no current to buck, and finding a firm gravel bottom for footing, he was across in four minutes. On the opposite bank he paused to look back. The huddle had broken up. Three of the pursuers had fanned out and were entering the tobacco field. The fourth was walking downhill toward the slough. It was the big man. McNair fingered the pistol in his pocket. *Buchanan,* he thought with some relish, *you're taking your last walk.*

He hurried into the forest, flayed at every turn by a whiplashing thicket. A quarter-mile later he was exhausted. He came to a fallen log, tested it to make sure it was solid, then crouched behind it and looked back toward the slough. He could no longer see it in the darkness. He shifted to a more comfortable sitting position and cocked his ear for any out-of-place sound. Even if Buchanan did have the guts to follow an armed man into woods like these—which McNair doubted—the big man would be at a disadvantage. With his bulk, he would bulldoze through the forest with all the grace of a stumbling hippopotamus. In that case, good ears were as important as good eyesight. And McNair had both. He opened the cylinder on his pistol, checked again to make sure it was fully loaded, and waited.

And waited.

The silence was broken only by the sound of night creatures stalking their prey. At the edge of the slough, water moccasins slithered toward unwary frogs. High above the trees, feeding bats folded their wings and dived unerringly between thick branches to feast on swarming insects. Now and then a great horned owl, alert for scampering rodents, hooted its eerie call. There were no sounds of man.

A mosquito landed on McNair's neck. He raised his hand to slap, caught the blunder, and rubbed the welt instead. A slap would have resounded through the woods—a sure giveaway to his hiding place. Or Buchanan's for that matter. *If* he was in the woods. The big man would also be plagued with insects. McNair listened for the tell-tale sounds of a man swatting bugs. None

50

came.

The sweltering, humid August heat of Kentucky, unbearable during the day, was worse at night. McNair's sweat-drenched shirt and trousers clung to his body like plaster casts. Perspiration matted his hair and stung his eyes. Merely to breath was a strain, like trying to inhale in a caldron. There was no breeze, no water to drink. No matter. He had the advantage. He was hard as nails from a regimen of a hundred push-ups a day and a five-mile run every morning before breakfast. The exercise wasn't vanity. It was insurance. And it had paid off more than once. So, however painful this night was to him, it was surely doubly so for his heavy, over-the-hill pursuer.

If Buchanan was in the woods.

The hours were leaden. McNair yearned to stand up, if only for a second, to stretch cramped muscles that screamed for relief. He didn't dare. This was a game of cat and mouse, sweat it out, suffer and win—and damned if he was going to be the mouse.

It was hours past the time when he should have left the woods. By now he should be driving a stolen car hell-bent for Fletcher Country. Well, that could be accomplished in daylight, too. Riskier, but not impossible. He would await dawn before moving. He rested his head against the log.

The cry of a great horned owl awoke him. Damn! A lapse like that could be a one-way ticket to hell. He leaned forward and grasped his legs with both hands and kneaded hard, working from his ankles to his hips, trying to revive his sluggish circulation. *Stay awake!* he admonished himself. *Buchanan may be in the woods.*

The soft gray light of dawn was just breaking over the tree tops when he heard a car start. One, or two? It must be the pursuers. It *had* to be!

He was elated. The Feds were falling back. He had hoodwinked them. Or had he? Perhaps they were retreating to arrange other roadblocks, or to bring in reinforcements. Or was it a trick? Was it only one man driving away in the car, leaving the others staked out to see if McNair would take the bait? His only option was to wait longer, to let the morning set in, to see how things looked in the clear light of day.

The sun was an hour high. McNair grasped his pistol and rose to a half-erect crouch. Slowly, warily, he turned and surveyed the forest in all directions. A steamy mist from the slough wafted among the trees like smoke from a hundred campfires and settled in the hollows. Overhead a chorus of bird songs greeted the new day. There was no sight or sound indicating the presence of another human.

With grim determination, he stood straight up, and waited. Minutes passed. Nothing. He stepped on a dry twig, purposely creating a sharp *snap!* Nothing. Relieved, he stretched his body long and hard. Then, gun in hand, he stepped around the log and started toward the slough.

Seventy-five feet from his hiding place a towering oak stood in his path. He skirted the huge tree, pushing aside the wild grape vines and ferns that grew at its base. On the other side of the oak he had a clear view of the slough. He'd taken two steps toward the water when a gruff voice startled him. "Drop that gun! Grab your head and don't turn around!"

McNair froze. Then in one fluid motion he wheeled and raised the gun. Before he could pull the trigger he saw the blur of an open hand coming at him. Next moment he was flying backward through the underbrush, as if he had been struck broadside with a sledgehammer.

When he regained consciousness he was lying on his back with his wrists hand-cuffed in front of him. Sitting on a nearby stump, the big man was looking through McNair's billfold. McNair moaned and raised himself up on one elbow.

The big man looked at him, then stood. "On your feet."

An excruciating pain seared McNair's jaw. Tears welled in his eyes. The son of a bitch had slapped him like he was some snot-nosed schoolboy. He hawked and spit toward his captor. "Screw you, Buchanan! You want me outa here you're going to have to carry me out."

He lay back defiantly.

Without a word, Buchanan walked over, grasped the handcuffs between McNair's wrist with one hand and started walking out of the forest, dragging the hapless prisoner as if he were no more than a sack of garbage. Jagged limbs and rocks ripped through McNair's clothing into his flesh. "All right, for God's sake!" he screamed. "I'll walk."

They left Frog Island without further incident.

Years later, when Jesse Buchanan was appointed warden at Eddyville, where McNair was serving time for bank robbery, the convict would share the story of Frog Island with selected cronies—never in praise of Buchanan, always in contempt.

Now, as he reflected on the past in the basement of the prison kitchen, he vowed that tomorrow he would show the world that the lionized warden was just another overrated jailer. Tomorrow he and his cohorts would bust out of the Kentucky State Penitentiary as if it were no more than a hick county slammer.

The second seating of the inmate line was filing into the dining hall for supper that Saturday afternoon when Robert McNair approached one of the servers. "Take a break, Gus. I'll handle it for a while."

Grateful, Gus handed the steel dipper to McNair and retreated to the basement to have a smoke.

While he ladled chili and beans onto the passing trays, McNair looked around the gymnasium-size room. Guard Roy Hogan was standing near the south wall, next to the large double doors that led out into the prison yard. Deputy Warden Ben Wilson was patrolling between the tables near the serving line. In accord with long-standing policy, both the deputy warden and the guard wore guns, even though there were inside the walls mingling with twelve hundred convicts. It was a practice Warden

Buchanan had considered rescinding, but hadn't done. Before the day was out, he would regret that he hadn't followed through on his instincts.

After a moment, McNair walked over to the dumbwaiter shaft and yelled down: "Dehart! Bring up another tray of bread."

Minutes later, Ezra Dehart placed a tray of bread near McNair and started running loaves through the electric slicer. Deputy Warden Wilson noticed that Earl Gibbs had accompanied Dehart and was standing idly near the serving line. Wilson approached the serving line. "Gibbs, you got no business up here. Get below."

Behind Wilson's back, McNair tore open a loaf of bread he had hollowed out the afternoon before and withdrew the contraband pistol. He grabbed Wilson from behind and stuck the pistol in the startled deputy's face. "Just keep calm, Wilson, and you won't get hurt. Ezra, get his gun."

Dehart took Wilson's gun from his holster.

All eating stopped. Around the room, three hundred sets of eyes stared incredulously at a drama often rumored in prisons but seldom attempted—an armed breakout.

Across the dining hall, Guard Hogan had a clear view of what was happening. His first reaction was to try to make it to the door and give an alarm. But even if he was successful he knew McNair wouldn't hesitate to shoot Wilson in retaliation. He drew his gun and started toward the armed convicts. Throughout the dining hall, inmates dived for cover beneath the tables. McNair pointed his gun and fired. The bullet hit Hogan high on the inside of his thigh. Hogan stumbled on, dragging his leg, but after a few more steps collapsed and rolled into a ball, moaning in agony. Blood spurted from the wound. Gibbs ran over and picked up his gun.

"Hey!" someone yelled, "this guy's bleeding bad."

"Let the son of a bitch bleed," McNair yelled back.

Working the serving line that day was a husky black cook known by his prison-circuit boxing name, "Big Train." Disregarding McNair's order, Big Train walked over to where Hogan lay bleeding his life away. Kneeling, Big Train turned

Hogan over onto his back, placed a hand high up in the stricken guard's groin and pressed the femoral artery hard against the pelvic bone. The spurting blood stopped.

While Dehart kept Wilson covered, McNair walked over and aimed his gun at Big Train's head. The husky cook stared back in defiance. The silence in the room was electric. After breathless seconds, McNair lowered the gun and turned away.

At 4:45 that afternoon, Porter Lady and Guard Clyde Twisdale had completed the lock-down of the shops inside the walls and were walking back across the prison yard to the administration building. Just then, a muffled *crack* came from the direction of the dining hall.

The two stopped. "Was that gunfire?" Lady asked.

Twisdale turned. "It sure sounded like it."

The dining hall was in the worst possible location for riot control. No wall tower had a clear view of it. With some stealth, a person could leave the rear door of the building, circle around to the north side, descend a low embankment, and approach within fifteen feet of the yard gate in the administration building before being spotted by the turnkey. No one was more aware of this flaw in prison security than Bob McNair. He had studied it for months. He also knew that the kitchen guard on the first floor, surrounded by constant din, would not be aware of what was happening in the dining room above. His shot, muffled by the thick walls and wooden fixtures, could have been heard only by someone passing close by. There was no evidence of that. The plan was proceeding exactly as he had envisioned it.

But the shot had been heard.

A gentle rise hid most of the dining hall from Lady and Twisdale's view. They ran across the grass toward the top of the knoll. All at once Lady grabbed Twisdale, pushed him to the ground, then dropped beside him. A hundred feet away four men had just emerged from the dining hall. Three were convicts. The fourth was Deputy Warden Ben Wilson. One of the convicts was holding what looked like a pistol at Wilson's back.

Anticipating the convicts' next move, Lady and Twisdale crawled along the knoll where they would have a clear view when the convicts emerged on the far side of the dining hall. Twisdale drew his .45 automatic pistol from his holster and checked to make sure there was a round in the chamber.

The convicts and their hostage were approaching the gate to the administration building. "Can you see who they are?" Lady asked.

"The guy herding Wilson in front of him is Bob McNair," Twisdale replied. "Earl Gibbs is with him. I can't make out that guy coming up behind. Looks like they each got a gun."

"Who's on turnkey?" Lady asked.

"Fred Jolly."

Lady remembered what Warden Buchanan had said about this eventuality. Every employee knew it. The yard gate would *not* be opened on demand of a convict for any reason. The warden had made it chillingly clear: "Not even if I am the hostage. They may force me to beg you to open the gate. *But you will not do it.*"

"He'll open it if Wilson asks him to," Lady despaired. "Sure as hell, he'll open it."

He lifted his head above the knoll. "McNair! This is Chief Lady. You're covered. Throw down those weapons and put your noses to the ground. Now!"

Bringing up the rear, Ezra Dehart, armed with Wilson's gun, stopped and fired toward the knoll. The bullet plowed into the ground two feet from Lady's head.

Steadying his .45 with both hands, Twisdale leveled it at Dehart, took a deep breath, and squeezed the trigger. The gun roared and jumped ten inches into the air. The half-inch-thick lead slug struck Dehart in the left hip and tore through his pelvis, exploding hundreds of jagged bone slivers throughout his abdomen. He slammed backward to the ground. Emitting a moan, he tried to rise, but couldn't. In a final act of defiance, he threw his gun across the ground to Gibbs. "Take this . . . and . . . bust out of . . . this stinking rat hole." They were the last words he ever spoke.

In the confusion of that moment, Deputy Warden Wilson broke from McNair's grasp and ran toward the open door of

Cellblock One, forty feet away. McNair shot once at the fleeing guard, but missed. He turned back to the gate, where Turnkey Jolly was standing with his key poised. McNair leveled the gun at Jolly. "Open it, Fred, or your wife's a widow tonight."

Jolly opened the gate.

From the knoll, Lady watched the gate swing open, as he'd predicted. The two remaining armed convicts entered the administration building. Lady turned to Twisdale. "Clyde, get to the dinning hall. Get things under control before this place blows all to hell. I've got to get around to the front before those guys do."

He broke into a run toward Wall Tower Six.

The wall tower guard had heard the shooting and had armed his rifle, but he couldn't see the action from his position. Then he saw Porter Lady come running across the yard. He was shouting something. The guard opened a window.

"Drop me your rifle!" Lady called out.

The guard stared. "Huh?"

Lady stopped directly beneath the tower. "Don't 'huh' me, dammit! Drop me your rifle! And sound the break alarm!"

The guard dropped the heavy .358-caliber Winchester rifle into Lady's arms, twenty-five feet below. Lady wheeled and ran downhill toward the south wall. As he came within earshot of the guard atop the truck gate tower he shouted, "Open the gate!"

The guard pushed a control, opening the double-wide truck gate that led to the outside.

"Grab the phone," Lady yelled as he raced through, repeating the order he'd given the previous wall tower guard. "Tell them to blow the wildcat whistle!"

He ran down the access road to the highway that ran in front of the prison. Three hundred yards ahead, the long-rising front steps of the prison were in plain view. He had to find cover somewhere at the bottom of those steps before McNair and Gibbs started down.

Just down the hill from the truck gate, Guard Sam Litchfield, walking toward the prison, saw Porter Lady, rifle in hand, emerge from the gate and run toward the front of the prison where he stooped behind the low wall bordering the sidewalk and stared intently at the steps leading down from the entrance. Litchfield sensed at once that someone was about to come down those front steps who shouldn't be there. He realized that if he remained on the walkway he would be a clear target for whoever that someone was.

Just off to Litchfield's right was the red brick home of Mr. and Mrs. Catlett, an elderly couple who had lived all their married life on their riverfront estate next to the prison. The two old people, unaware of what was taking place, were sitting on their front porch. Ida Catlett waved to Litchfield. "Good afternoon, Sam."

To the couple's surprise, Litchfield left the sidewalk, raced across their yard and began to beat his way through a privet hedge on the north side of the house. "Go inside!" he yelled. "Lock your doors and stay there!"

The Catletts fled to the security of their home.

Clearing the hedge, Litchfield ran in a crouch along the sidewalk wall toward Porter Lady.

Inside the administration building, Bob McNair grabbed the key ring from Turnkey Fred Jolly's hand an relocked the yard gate. He didn't want a bunch of cons streaming through and screwing up his plan. He turned to Jolly. "Which one of these keys opens the gun box?"

The gun box was a closet-size cabinet in the hallway near the front gate.

"Hunt for it," Jolly replied.

McNair cocked his pistol and stuck it in Jolly's nose. "Are you sure you wouldn't rather tell me?"

"The brass one," Jolly said.

McNair opened the gun box. He stuck two .38-caliber Colt Police Special revolvers in his belt, filled his pockets with ammunition, then had Gibbs do the same.

"Bob, why hasn't the alarm sounded?" Gibbs asked nervously.

"Just thank God for small favors, Earl," McNair replied. "Cover Fred for a minute."

He left Gibbs with Turnkey Jolly and walked down the hallway of the administration building, stopping to look into each office. Convict clerks stared at him blankly. He ordered them to stay put.

At the last office, he stood with his back to the officers barber shop, just across the hall. Alone in the shop, where he had been waiting for the prison barber to return from supper, Guard Nelson Cramer, 69, pulled out his .38 revolver and pointed it at McNair's back. He stood that way for several seconds. McNair turned, saw the gun leveled at him and looked steadily at Cramer. A wet spot appeared in the crotch of Cramer's pants.

McNair said, "You gonna shoot that thing, Cramer, or just stand there pissing in your pants?"

Cramer's hand began to shake. McNair stepped over and took the gun. "Now, you stay here, old man, you hear? If I see you out in the hall I'm gonna blast your ass away."

Cramer dropped into a chair and nodded.

McNair returned to the main coridor gate, unlocked it and motioned Gibbs and Jolly through.

Ahead of them lay the long front corridor, the front steps, and, just across the highway, the parking lot where McNair planned to hot-wire a car and speed southward to the Tennessee border. Once in Tennessee, he'd head eastward through the Cumberland Mountains to Letcher County, Kentucky, and freedom.

At the front door, McNair ordered Fred Jolly to get in front of them. "Just stay calm, Fred, and nothing will happen to you. Soon as we get across the road to the cars we'll let you go. Now, walk on, careful-like."

Porter Lady had been stationed at his refuge behind the low wall for only a few minutes when he spotted Guard Sam Litchfield crawling up the sidewalk toward him. Litchfield, a renowned hunter who had been known to bring down a quail on the wing with a .22 rifle, was the best sharpshooter on the guard force. Lady drew his pistol, then motioned Litchfield to his side and handed him the rifle. "There're two of them, Sam, both armed. They'll be coming down the steps any time now, maybe with hostages. We can't let them get across to the cars."

Just then, the stillness was shattered by an earsplitting, undulating sound coming from atop the power house inside the prison walls. Known as the "wildcat whistle," the shrill, steam-driven alarm was a warning to the countryside that something was wrong at the prison.

By coincidence, at that moment, Warden Buchanan, with his wife and two youngest children in the car, had arrived back in Eddyville from Owensboro and was just starting up the long hill leading to the prison. At the sound of the wildcat whistle, he made a sharp veer to the side of the road in front of the Prince Hardware Store, stopped the engine, and ordered his family to remain in the car. Jumping out, he began to run uphill toward the institution.

Porter Lady spotted the armed convicts first. Peeping over the low wall, he saw McNair push Jolly out the front door and start descending the steps. Gibbs was close behind.

"He's got Fred," Lady said to Litchfield.

Lady looked up and down the highway. On both sides of the prison, guards alerted by the alarm were flagging down cars to keep them from driving into the danger zone. Lady took a deep breath. Fixing his eyes on the guns in the convicts' hands, he stood.

"McNair! Gibbs! At this moment you are in the gunsights of guards in front and on both sides of you. Your position is hopeless. Release your hostage and surrender your weapons while you still have your lives."

It was a daring bluff. The only other armed person between the felons and the parking lot was Sam Litchfield.

McNair raised his gun toward Porter Lady. With a bone-jolting thud, Lady dropped to the sidewalk just as McNair fired. The bullet tore a hole in the asphalt on the highway behind Lady.

Just outside the prison waterworks, fifty feet off to one side of the front steps, convict Macon Talbot had become an unwilling witness to the drama unfolding before him. He had just unloaded several crates of water purification alum from the back of the prison pickup truck and was about to return to the Eddyville depot for another load. Spotting Chief of Staff Lady and Guard Litchfield on the street below, and the armed convicts on the steps above, Macon realized that he was caught smack in the middle of what was going to be one hell of a shoot-out. He jumped into the cab of the truck and sat there, wondering what to do next.

Then one of the convicts shot at Porter Lady, and Macon threw himself down on the seat.

Macon's dive for cover caught McNair's eye. He knew who the cowering trusty was. "Talbot! Get off your black ass and get that truck over here pronto."

Macon rose slowly to a sitting position and sat there without moving.

McNair swung his pistol toward the truck. "Now, Talbot!"

Macon wondered if McNair could hit him from that distance. He made a show of turning the ignition key without actually stepping on the accelerator. The starter motor whirred, but didn't turn over. Macon kept his foot off the gas. The motor ground out several more revolutions and quit. Macon looked up at McNair and spread his arms signifying that it was useless.

"You son of a bitch!" McNair yelled, and fired. The truck windshield shattered. Macon fell sideways in the seat.

McNair turned back toward the street. "Lady! Call off your goons. Get one of those cars started and back away with your hands up, else you're going to see your friend Jolly's brains scattered all over these steps."

He put the gun to Jolly's head and started down the steps.

Porter Lady thought quickly. He knew McNair well. The man was ruthless, far more so than some of the inmates who had been executed. He wouldn't hesitate to kill Jolly.

He looked over at Litchfield. The guard's reputation as a marksman was well known. Lady wondered if he was good enough to bring down McNair without hitting Jolly.

Lady said, "Sam, get a bead on that bastard. I'm going to try to draw him away."

Litchfield took aim, sucked in and released a couple of deep breaths, and held the rifle steady.

Lady cocked his pistol and stood up again. As Lady hoped he would do, McNair lowered his gun from Jolly's head and pointed it at Lady. Unexpectedly seizing the moment, Fred Jolly broke from McNair's grasp and ran for his life toward the shelter of a tree in the yard just below the steps. Startled, McNair fired once at the fleeing guard, missed, then turned and fired at Lady. Still standing, Lady returned fire twice, striking McNair in the side and arm.

McNair didn't budge. "You lousy son of a bitch!" he screamed. Pulling another gun from his belt, he aimed both at Lady.

At that moment, Litchfield's Winchester roared. McNair's body flew backward as if he had been hit by a sledgehammer. The .358 slug tore through his chest, splitting his heart in two. He was dead before he hit the steps.

For a breathless moment, Earl Gibbs stood with his gun dangling at his side, staring down at McNair's shattered body. Then he dropped the weapon, threw himself face forward onto the steps and screamed, "Don't shoot me! Please! Don't shoot me!"

In the end, it was Bob McNair's fatal misjudgment that thwarted his desperate bid for freedom. He had not suspected that he would come up against three officials that day who were every bit as formidable in a fight as Jesse Buchanan had been that night on Frog Island—three officials, the warden would always recall with pride, whom only months before he had saved from being tossed onto the scrap heap of power politics.

Buchanan arrived at the top of the hill just as Earl Gibbs was begging for mercy. Porter Lady briefed the warden on what had happened. Assured that the uprising had been quelled, Buchanan ran to the waterworks, where the Chevrolet truck with the bullet-shattered windshield was sitting ominously still. Yanking the door open, he grabbed Macon Talbot's wrist, feeling for a pulse. It was throbbing as strong as a jack hammer.

"Macon . . . are you playing possum?"

Macon opened one eye, cautiously. "That you, Warden?"

"It's me. You can get up now."

Macon made no effort to move. "I don't know. You sure, now?"

The warden dropped Macon's arm. "Why you suspicious old coot. Stay there all day if you want. I've got work to do."

He sent a guard to get his family, then went to his office, where for the remainder of that afternoon and evening he took statements from officials and convicts involved in the attempted break. By midnight, he had arrived at some vital decisions. In his labored, barely decipherable scrawl, he made notes of the actions he would recommend or announce the following day:

— Nominate Porter Lady, Clyde Twisdale, and Sam Litchfield for Certificate of Merit. Request merit pay raise.
— Authorize state funding of Ray Hogan's medical bills.
— Reassign Fred Jolly from turnkey to regular guard duty. New turnkey: Clyde Twisdale.
— Promote Sam Litchfield to Yard Captain.
— Transfer Nelson Cramer to State Highway Department.
— Send smuggled gun to State Attorney for investigation, possible indictments.
— Recommend Governor Chandler commute sentence of Convict Big Train to time served.

In another vital decision that he knew now he had put off too long, he rescinded the order allowing guards to carry firearms inside the prison walls. The unpopular decision soon proved its worth. The McNair riot was the last time during Buchanan's long tenure as warden that an inmate attempted to shoot his way out of the Kentucky State Penitentiary.

7

Henry Sproule plugged in the coffee pot beside his desk in the anteroom just outside Warden Buchanan's office, then returned to the notes he'd compiled for the warden's morning staff meeting. A slender, small-built, sandy-haired man in his mid-thirties, Sproule wore the white-shirt, khaki-trousers uniform of an office trustee. Once chief clerk in a major investment firm in Louisville, he was now serving time for embezzlement. He had been Warden Buchanan's personal secretary for five years. Perusing the notes, Sproule glanced again at the date on his calendar. It was going to be a hectic day. The day of an execution was always difficult. The work went on, jobs got done, but the grim awareness of what the approaching night would bring hung like a pall over the institution. And today, Sproule mused with glum resignation, would surely be the worst. The execution of the Miley murderers. If anything could push the war news off the front pages, that would do it.

Reporters were already beginning to arrive, much earlier in the day than ever before. Sproule didn't care much for reporters—with good reason. It was an investigative reporter following up on rumors about his opulent lifestyle who brought Sproule to the bar of justice. From that day on he had refused to read a newspaper, embracing historical novels instead. What news he did follow, primarily about the war, he garnered from the radio in his cell or from chit-chat with visitors to the warden's office.

He checked again to make sure he had Governor Johnson's itinerary for the next sixteen hours. He had it, as he knew he did before looking. But on days like today, when lives hung in the balance, it was always wise to check things twice, then twice again. The governor would be in his office at the Capitol in Frankfort, or home in the mansion, throughout the day and night. At mid-morning, and again that evening, Sproule would call the phone company to remind them to keep a line free that night between Frankfort and Eddyville, just in case. He would call to release the line after it was no longer needed.

At precisely nine o'clock, Porter Lady came through the door. Following the resignation of Deputy Warden Wilson soon after the McNair episode, Warden Buchanan had abolished the position of Chief of Staff and appointed Lady as the new Deputy Warden. He had served in that position ever since.

Sproule stood when the deputy entered. "Warden says for you to go right in, sir."

Lady rapped on the jam of the warden's open door and stepped inside. The office was spacious but sparsely appointed. A brown leather couch with chrome arms sat against one wall. Matching chairs sat facing the warden's plain oak desk. The desk bore assorted papers, a pen set mounted on a white marble base, a phone with two private lines, a pipe rack cradling a collection of briars and meerschaums, a humidor filled with Kentucky Club tobacco, and a tightly closed jar containing White Owl Panatella cigars.

Seated at his desk, the warden was dressed in brown tweed trousers, a tan tie, and a white monogrammed shirt with the sleeves rolled up at the wrists. His suit coat, hat, and cane hung on a rack near the door. He was not a desk man and spent as little time as possible in his office. Already that morning he had inspected the dining hall and kitchen, the infirmary, the shop areas, and the new cellblock recently constructed at his insistence. He had also made his first visit of the day to the three men scheduled for execution that night. By law, he would be required to visit them at least once more before the time of their executions.

Deputy Warden Lady sat down in one of the chairs and watched the warden peel a Winesap apple with his pocket knife, letting the dark red peels drop onto his desk blotter. When the apple was clean, he picked up one of the peels and packed it into the humidor along with the tobacco, then placed another in the jar with the cigars. He sliced off a piece of apple and handed it to Lady, who took it. The warden bit into the remainder.

Sproule entered with coffee, handed a cup to the warden and deputy, then took his place in a side chair with a fold-up arm for writing.

The warden dropped the apple core into the waste basket. "No one else attending today?"

"No sir," Sproule replied.

"All right. Let's get on with it."

Sproule opened his pad. He had culled the notes for today, eliminating items that could be postponed. He knew that the warden would insist on meeting with any employee or convict that asked, but, barring an emergency, they could wait. There were far more consequential matters the warden had to attend to today.

Sproule looked at the pad. "Mr. Ingels called early. The moving van's coming this morning and he wanted to know if you found anything for him yet. He seems to be pretty depressed."

The warden frowned at his oversight. He should have called Ingels last evening.

For two years Ingels had been a guard-in-residence at one of the prison farms. One morning the previous week he had returned home at mid-morning unexpected. As he pulled up in front of his house he spotted one of the farm pickup trucks parked in the rear. He was puzzled. The convict driver had no business on this side of the farm. As Ingles walked toward the house, the truck driver ran out the back door, jumped in his truck and raced away. When Ingels entered the house, the look on his wife's face was an indisputable indictment to what had occurred. In a tearful confession, she admitted that it wasn't the first time.

Realizing that his position was irreparably compromised, Ingels drove to the prison that morning, reported the incident to the warden, and submitted his resignation.

It wasn't a common infraction, but such indiscretions did occur. Like priests, prison trustees were an enticing temptation to women who couldn't resist forbidden fruit.

The warden had accepted Ingels's resignation without prejudice. The convict involved was confined to his cell for thirty days and lost trustee status.

The warden said to Sproule: "Tell Ingels to report to the State Highway Department office in Madisonville Monday morning. There'll be a job for him there."

Sproule made a note.

"Senator Glenn's secretary called early this morning," he continued. "The senator has assured Morris Hayden that there'll be no problem in him getting two passes for the executions tonight. He wants to make certain the pass will be ready when Mister Hayden gets here."

The warden scowled. "Wants to make certain, does he?"

A one-time coal miner, now a radio evangelist, Morris Hayden was well known throughout the midwest and south. Starting with a tent ministry after being injured in a mine accident, he had parlayed a hellfire-and-brimstone style into a widespread following of "prayer partners" numbering in the hundreds of thousands. He owned his own radio station, as well as vast holdings in real estate. His popularity with listeners equated to power, and he was both courted and feared by politicians. He had no relationship, secular or clerical, with any of the three men scheduled to die this night.

The warden said, "Call the senator's secretary back and tell her to inform her boss that I said this is a serious affair, not some damned three-ringed circus. No passes for Hayden."

Deputy Warden Lady smiled uneasily. "Warden, Senator Glenn is a powerful man."

"I'll take care of Senator Glenn, Porter."

The warden looked at Sproule. "Next."

Sproule glanced at his pad. "Senator McKellar's letter requested a response by the first of next week. You'll have to get it in the mail by tomorrow morning for it to get to Washington on time."

The warden frowned. He'd been procrastinating on the matter for over a week.

Kenneth McKellar, U.S. Senator from Tennessee, was planning to introduce a sweeping penal reform bill in the current Congress. Senator Alban Barkley of Kentucky had suggested that Warden Buchanan's support for the anti–capital punishment provision would carry great weight with the legislators.

The warden said, "I'd do most anything for Alban Barkley. But the McKellar Bill . . . ?"

He turned reflective. "You know, Ruby LaFoon and McKellar are peas in a pod on this anti–capital punishment thing. Governor LaFoon was one of the finest gentlemen I ever met. We saw eye-to-eye on most things. But he was quick to commute death sentences for scoundrels who should have been hung the day they were captured. I don't know how Alban got the idea that I'd support McKellar on something like that." He thought for a long while. "No, prepare a letter to the senator for my signature. Tell him thanks, I'm honored that he'd ask me, and so forth. But explain that I just can't get behind him on this one."

Sproule made another note.

He pulled a sheet of paper from where he'd folded it in the pad and handed it to the warden. "This was in yesterday's outgoing. The mail censors asked me to bring it up this morning."

71

The warden unfolded the paper. It was a explicit four-color drawing of a man and woman engaged in sexual intercourse. A barred window in the background and the cot beneath the pair were exact replicas of those in the prison cells. Artistically first-rate, the sketch was evidence of creative painstaking. More telling, the woman in the drawing was a mirror image of the youngest of the two female mail censors at the institution.

As in any prison, pornographic writing, often vividly illustrated with elaborate drawings, was a fact of life at Eddyville. Fantasy was the nearest most inmates ever got to a woman. Most of the convicts kept the prurient material hidden from officials, trading scripts and drawings among themselves. In many prisons, officials simply ignored the practice—some even considered it healthy. But there was always a deviant among the practitioners, and the two female censors at Eddyville were the most vulnerable targets.

The warden handed the drawing to Deputy Lady. "Another sick one. See if Woodward can trace it."

Tom Woodward was the Bertillon Chief at the prison. He was responsible for making positive identification of all persons sentenced to or released from the institution. His expertise with fingerprints was legendary, and he was often called on to assist the Federal Bureau of Investigation in the investigation of federal crimes in the area. Still, both the warden and the deputy knew that the chances of him identifying the offender in the porno case were slim.

"Anything else?" the warden asked.

Sproule stood to leave. "You asked me to remind you about Macon Talbot."

The warden's face clouded. "Yes. I want to see him in here just as soon as the deputy warden and I are finished."

"Yes sir." Sproule left, closing the door behind him.

Warden Buchanan picked up a folder from his in-basket. Porter Lady took a notebook and pen from his pocket. The warden scanned the duty roster of guards who had assisted at past executions. All executions were attended by the warden, the death house supervisor, the night captain of the guards, the prison physician, and other prison officials the warden requested. Visitors passes were granted on a restricted basis to reporters, ministers requested by the condemned, and, on request, to family members of victims of the condemned, who wanted to see vengeance extracted with their own eyes. Witnesses requested by the condemned were sometimes approved.

Execution duty was once rotated among the full guard force. As a result, excellent guards, willing to perform any duty except that, had resigned. To stem such losses, Warden Buchanan revised the duty to voluntary. The change hadn't made the selection any easier. Some volunteers became dangerously distracted for days following an execution. They were removed from the volunteer list without prejudice. Others, over-eager to perform the duty, were just as swiftly removed. Those remaining on the volunteer list comprised three-forths of the force. They were assigned execution duty on a rotating basis with certain stalwarts being favored. It was from among these stalwarts that the warden selected four men.

Lady jotted down the names.

The warden picked up the visitors pass list. There were forty-three names, thirty-five of them reporters from around the country—the largest media coverage of an execution in Kentucky history.

The warden studied one of the names on the list, puzzled. "What's Father Libs's name doing here? Last I heard, Tom wasn't speaking to him. Doesn't Tom want Father Donnelly?"

"Donnelly's on active duty with the army and can't get away," Lady explained. "It's Libs or nobody, and Tom isn't about to die without a priest at his side."

"I see. Have Anderson or Baxter requested ministers?"

"Not that I know of. Reverend Chandler has been meeting with them every day, but I don't know how it's coming along."

Reverend L. I. Chandler was the official prison chaplain. In all cases where condemned men did not request a personal pastor to be with them on their final day, he would minister to them at their request or simply stand by in case of a last-minute appeal for his services.

Lady said, "I'm not even sure Willie truly understands what's going on."

The warden agreed. Baxter was a hop-head, a ne'er-do-well, but those were hardly capital crimes. "Make sure Reverend Chandler's down there tonight," he said, "just in case."

The warden pulled a desk pen from its holder, wrote "Approved" at the bottom of the list, and initialed it. He handed the list to the deputy. The deputy took the list and nodded toward a photo of the warden's family on the credenza behind his desk. "How's Bill's research coming?"

Bill was the warden's son. His "research" was a topic of interest at the prison and beyond. Beginning in his sophomore year in high school, he had conducted in-depth interviews with every man confined to the death house, sometimes conversing until the moment the man was escorted to the death chamber. He hoped to use the material in a planned career in criminology. In the past year he had concentrated on the Miley murders.

"The notebook's getting thicker," the warden replied. "Penney and Baxter have revealed some interesting things about their personal life. Anderson hasn't told him much . . . except that he's been railroaded."

The warden gave a faint chuckle. "Bill has asked me to keep his notes in the safe when he goes into the army. Reckon that's the least I can do."

He pushed back his chair and stood. Turning to the huge barred window behind his desk, he placed his hands in his hip pockets and stared for several minutes across the street in front of the prison to the river, a quarter-mile away. Muddy from the beginning pre-spring run-off, the Cumberland was overflowing its banks, presaging flood conditions. There was fear of another disaster like the '37 flood, which nearly destroyed the town. The prison, secure on high ground, was untouched. A number of displaced families from town were sheltered and fed at the institution until the waters receded.

Deputy Warden Lady watched the warden silently. He had seen that sober stance before. There was something on the warden's mind, and he wanted to talk it out. The deputy waited.

"Porter," the resonant southern voice spoke at last, "what's your opinion . . . your honest-to-God gut feelings about Bob Anderson?"

Lady had expected that this would be the topic. He'd sensed the warden's uneasiness about Anderson for days. "I think he's a mighty cool customer, that he has two of the sharpest lawyers in the business, and that he's guilty as hell."

The warden chuckled at Lady's candor. Each passing year confirmed the wisdom of making Porter his deputy. He returned to his desk and sat down. "And Penney?"

"Brilliant in many ways. Self-educated. Ornery at one time, now seemingly contrite. Certainly obsessed with death house religion."

"Don't mock death house religion," the warden admonished. "Remember Dismas?"

"Dismas?"

"The repentant thief at the Crucifixion—Penney's idol. Dismas was the classic conversion of a condemned criminal. And that's exactly what's gnawing at my insides about tonight. Let's look at what we have here. Now, Father Donnelly is one of the wisest men of the cloth I've ever met, and he's convinced that Tom Penney is a sincere convert. All right, let's say Donnelly is right."

He leaned forward to tally points on his fingers. "Then the facts of the matter are these: one, a year ago Tom Penney, the scoffing heathen, the unrepentant murderer, fingered Bob Anderson as his accomplice and the trigger man in the Miley killings; two, a year later, Tom Penney, the born-again Christian, recants and says that Anderson is innocent; three, now he refuses to say another word about the case."

He sat back, his countenance revealing genuine concern. "That's what's disturbing me, Porter. Which Tom Penney told the truth—the heathen or the Christian?"

It was an argument that had been debated in legal circles and the media for months and would be repeated in a final appeal in the governor's office by Anderson's lawyers this morning. The deputy wished he could say something to ease the warden's burden. Instead, he asked, "Which story do you believe, Warden?"

The warden disregarded the question. "I went to see Bob this morning. I thought there might be some change in him today. There isn't. He's unshakable. Swears that Penney has railroaded him. He admits he's no angel . . . and hell, we all know he's as crooked as a snake's back. But he swore to me again this morning that he's no killer."

The warden gazed into the middle distance. "You know, Abe Lincoln used to tell a story about a vigilante group who strung up the wrong boy. When they learned their mistake they cut the lad's body down and carried it to his mother. 'Well,' they told the grieving woman, 'the joke's sure on us.'

"That's not the sort of 'joke' I want on my conscience, Porter."

Lady wanted to say that it wasn't really the warden's responsibility. He was merely part of the system, an instrument of the state. But he knew murmuring platitudes wouldn't help. Instead, he said, "I'm going down to get things set up with Captain Rankin in a few minutes. Penney goes first, right?"

On the occasion of multiple executions the order of priority, established by law, was the order of conviction. First sentenced, first to die. Under that rule, the order of executions for this night should have been Anderson, Penney, Baxter. Weeks before, the warden had petitioned the governor in secret for authority to put Penney first. In the electric chair, the warden explained, faced with his final moments to make peace with God, Penney might reveal which of his conflicting testimonies about Anderson was the truth. It was a long shot, but it could possibly save an innocent man's life. Though it was of questionable legality, Governor Johnson approved the tactic. His endorsement afforded the plan an extra edge of legitimacy in case the courts later questioned it.

Soon after making the deal with the governor, the warden had briefed Lady about the change. Now the warden shook his head. "No. We'll follow the legal order of execution."

Lady's face registered surprise.

"I realize it's another switch," the warden said, "but I've got my reasons. I haven't told you about it before, but Penney asked to see me late one night just before he clammed up. I don't want to say more about that now. But I'll tell you this. I got the feeling that he was counting on dying first; it was almost as if he had read my mind. I've given that a lot of thought. If Tom *wants* to go first tonight, why? It puzzled me for a while; I couldn't get a handle on it. But now I think I know his reason. And I'm not going to play by his rules. No . . . right or wrong, Anderson goes first. And I'll tell you something else; if what *could* happen tonight because of Anderson going first *does* happen, I'm going to stop everything on the spot and throw this whole ungodly mess right back into the court's lap."

It was too cryptic for Lady. But if that's the way the warden wanted it, that's the way it would be. "I'll brief Captain Rankin," he said.

"Only him," the warden said. "Absolutely no one else."

"Yes sir."

After a moment, the warden added, "Porter, this is one part of the job where you don't gain confidence with experience. It doesn't get any easier. If you ever sit at this desk, and I'm betting you will some day, I hope you find a better way to come to grips with it than I have."

Macon Talbot stood at a semblance of attention in front of the warden's desk. Every few seconds he shifted from one foot to the other, twisted his bill cap in his hands, and leaned forward in an attempt to see what paper in the thick inmate file the warden was studying now.

"Damn it, Macon," the warden exclaimed, "sit down. You're making me nervous."

"Yes Sir, Warden. I'll just sit right over here . . . close by."

He flopped into the deep leather cushion of the nearest chair and began to drum his fingernails noisily on the chrome armrest.

The warden closed the file in disgust. He knew it by heart anyway. "Macon, how many years have you spent in prison?"

Macon's brow knitted. "How many? Lessee now . . . thirty?"

"Thirty-three," the warden said.

"Thirty-three. That a fact? Thirty-three years. Reckon that's some kinda record, huh, warden?" Macon's pleasant coffee-colored face broke into an ear-to-ear grin.

"No, it's not a record. And it's nothing to be proud of. It's a damned shame."

The grin turned to a deep frown and Macon nodded in quick agreement. "Yes Sir. That's what it is, all right. Damn shame . . . that's the word for it."

Fifty-three-year-old Macon Talbot first went to reform school at age fourteen for burglarizing a dairy warehouse in his hometown of Sturgis. Released when he was twenty-one, he drifted to Frankfort, where he worked off and on as a janitor and handyman in the state capitol. When he was twenty-three he burglarized a bakery on Washington Street and was sentenced to ten years in the old state prison at Frankfort. Eight years later he was released on parole to a coal mine operator in Madisonville. He worked in the mines for six months. After his shift one night he stole a truck loaded with coal and drove to Paducah and tried to sell the truck and its load to a fuel broker who happened to be his boss's nephew. He was sentenced to ten years in the maximum security prison at Eddyville. Denied parole, he served out his time. Six months later he was arrested in Louisville for car theft. Sentenced this time under the Habitual Criminal Act, he was sent to Eddyville for life.

In 1936, to the dismay of prison officials, the new warden, Jesse Buchanan, made Talbot an outside trustee, assigned to maintain and drive the institution's green Chevrolet pickup truck. One year later Buchanan's judgment was vindicated when Talbot refused at gunpoint to surrender the truck to Bob McNair during McNair's ill-fated attempt to escape.

For six years Macon hauled supplies to and from the prison farms, ran errands around the country, drove the warden's children to school, and went wherever else he was sent. He came and went alone.

In Kentucky, a lifer was eligible for parole in eight years. In December 1942, with a model record as an outside trustee, Macon

Talbot was once again set free. That Christmas Eve, Warden Buchanan drove him to the Eddyville depot to catch the Illinois Central passenger train to Louisville. At the station, the warden asked, "How much money you got, Macon?"

Macon pulled forth a battered clasp-locked change purse and counted. As a working trustee he had been paid eight cents a day for the past six years. A nickel of that had gone each day for a sack of tobacco, the remaining three cents had been deposited into his inmate savings account.

"I got . . . sixty-two dollars, and . . . twenty-three cents."

The warden handed him another twenty-five dollars, ten from the state and fifteen from his own pocket. "This is your last chance to make it on the outside, Macon. You have a good job lined up with that maintenance shop, and I've personally vouched for you. Now, I don't want to see you in this part of the state ever again. Understand?"

"Yes sir, Mister Buchanan. I understand. Don't you worry none. I learned my lesson good this time. You wont be seein' me down thisaway never no more. No sir . . . never."

And Macon Talbot caught the train to Louisville.

Five weeks later Macon took the streetcar from his boarding house on South Third to downtown Louisville. He got off at Fourth and Broadway and started walking slowly north on Fourth, looking into the windows of parked cars. In front of Stewarts Department Store he spotted a Dodge coupe with the keys still in the ignition. He got in, started the engine, let it idle for a while, then pulled out into traffic. All that afternoon and the next day he cruised up and down Fourth Street near Stewarts. No one stopped him.

The third day he parked in a No Parking zone across the street from the store and sat there all morning. Nothing happened.

On the fourth day, desperate, he pulled in behind a police cruiser as it drove away from the station and followed it for several blocks until it stopped for a red light. Floorboarding the accelerator, he rammed into the back of the cruiser, sorely shaking up two of Louisville's finest.

That did it.

Tried a second time under the Habitual Criminal Act, Macon was again sentenced to life in prison at Eddyville. He re-entered the penitentiary on February 11, 1943, two weeks before the meeting this morning with Warden Buchanan.

"Macon," the warden said, "if the state's going to pay your keep, you're going to have to share the load."

"Yes sir," Macon agreed. "That's the way it oughta be."

The warden opened his desk drawer and pulled out a set of keys. He pitched them to Macon. "That old Chevy truck's sitting out front by the waterworks. Never has run right since you left."

Macon grabbed the keys in mid-air and jumped to his feet. "Don't you worry none, Warden. I'm gonna have it purrin' like a kitty cat in no time . . . no time a'tall."

He started to leave.

"Macon."

"Yes sir?"

"There won't be any more paroles."

Macon's brow knitted. "No sir . . . I reckon not." He looked at the keys in his hand, broke into a wide grin, and left.

Macon Talbot was home.

9

The westbound bus, plagued with interminable small-town stops and a 35-mile-per-hour wartime speed limit, took an agonizing seven hours to cover the 197 miles between Louisville and Eddyville. On any other occasion, the thin, sallow-complexioned woman seated next to the window near the rear emergency exit could not have cared less where she was going. But today was different. Ever since leaving the Jefferson Street station at 7:00 A.M. Pearl Smith wondered if she wanted to reach the end of this journey at all. Still, she knew she had to do it, had to keep a promise she had made many months before.

She pulled the chin strap of the yellow kerchief that covered her dyed black hair tighter and looked out the window at the winter-still countryside. The darkened sky cast a pall that matched her mood. A sudden reflection in the window gave her a start until she realized it was her own face. She raised a hand to her cheek. The stress of the past months had aged her far beyond her years.

She purposely turned her attention to her fellow passengers. Most were in uniform, soldiers and sailors going on or returning from leave. One could see them everywhere these days—on buses, on trains, hitchhiking along the highways. She studied the soldier seated beside her. He was what most women would call handsome, and he was sound asleep. She noticed the chevrons of a master sergeant on his tunic, and an old resentment stirred in her. No, she resolved. Let that sleeping dog lie. She laid her head back and closed her eyes. She wasn't sleepy. But she was tired of looking at soldiers. She'd had enough of soldiers to last her a lifetime.

Eddyville, Kentucky, population 1,200, excluding convicts, lay sprawled in rural non-conformity along U.S. 62 in the verdant Cumberland River Valley of Lyon County. There was no official bus stop. Passengers caught the bus anywhere they could flag down the driver. The single exception was the River View Inn, a small cafe adjacent to the state parking lot atop the hill, just across the road from the penitentiary. Opened years before by a sharp-eyed businessman who counted the number of passengers who disembarked at Eddyville every day solely to visit inmate relatives, the tiny restaurant had become the town's unofficial bus stop.

On this chilly February afternoon two men and one woman got off the 1:00 P.M. westbound bus. From behind the counter just inside the cafe, owner Archie Barrett studied the new arrivals through the window. He had been doing that for years and could pretty well guess which passengers were there to visit the prison on business and which ones were relatives of inmates. The two men, relatively well dressed, though rumpled from the long ride, had the look of reporters down to cover the executions that night, Barrett figured. The woman was wearing dark slacks, a plain black cloth coat, and a yellow kerchief around her head. She was thin to the point of emaciation, with a coarse, hard-life look about her. He wondered if she was a relative of one of the condemned men, come for a final farewell.

As the bus pulled away, the two men stretched long and hard for a moment, then grabbed their bags and crossed the road to the institution. The woman stood for a long while in the parking lot, as if trying to decide what to do next.

Pearl Smith felt utterly alone. She watched her fellow departing passengers cross the road toward the prison, then turned her gaze to that massive stone and steel structure that dominated the skyline for miles in every direction. She hadn't known what to expect. Now, seeing the Kentucky State Penitentiary for the first time, she felt mixed emotions. There was—she was reluctant to admit it—an awesome magnificence about the place. She found herself wishing she could have seen it first in summer, when its pampered bluegrass lawns, huge oaks, maples, and dogwoods, and countless well-pruned shrubs would have been in full bloom.

Centered in this pastoral setting between outreaching wings of cellblocks was the towering administration building. The imposing structure, every massive limestone block crafted precisely in place, didn't fit Pearl's notion of how a prison should look. It reminded her more of . . . what? A castle? No. A cathedral. That was it. A medieval British countryside cathedral, like those she had seen in the movies and in travel brochures. The rugged attraction of the place certainly belied its purpose.

After a moment, she turned and entered the cafe.

She gave a perfunctory nod to the man behind the counter and approached a table by the window. From one side of the table she would have a view of the prison. From the other side, the river. She chose the river view.

She removed her coat and placed it on the opposite chair and sat down. She left the kerchief around her head. Bone weary from the exhausting trip, she took a deep breath and tried to relax. There was a pleasant, clean smell about the place. The hardwood floor, yellow plastered walls, and hardwood counter looked freshly scrubbed. The red-and-white checkered tablecloths were faded from many launderings, but spotless. She glanced casually at the only other patron in the cafe, a middle-aged man eating a hamburger at a table against the wall. He was dressed in some sort of dark uniform. It came to her that he must be a prison guard.

There was a hand-printed menu wedged between the sugar dispenser and the napkin holder. Pearl picked it up, looked it over for a moment, then put it back in place. The man behind the counter stepped out and came to the table.

"Help you, Miss?"

"Just coffee. Cream, if you have it."

"I've got canned milk."

"That's fine." It wasn't, but she was getting used to it.

She looked out the window toward the river. She had grown up on the banks of the Ohio River near Cincinnati and liked rivers. To the west, the Cumberland meandered a serpentine course through rich bottom-land farms framed by dense, wooded hills. Just below the cafe, at the foot of a limestone cliff, were a dam and locks, navigation aids to the barge-laden boats that plied between harborfront cities along the Cumberland. On this day, in the face of a heavy run-off, the center section of dam wickets were lowered and a mighty cascade of white water spilled through, forming eddies that churned and agitated the river for miles. The ever-present eddies had given the town its name.

Her coffee arrived. She poured in a good portion of canned milk, which the man who served her had decanted into a small china pitcher, omitted sugar, then stirred well and took a sip. She was mildly surprised to find the coffee quite good, full-bodied and freshly brewed. Perhaps it would revive her.

After a while she noticed the clock above the counter and remembered that she was now in the Central Time Zone. She set her watch back an hour. She thought of the long afternoon and evening that lay ahead before it would be time to . . . to do what she had come to do.

She heard the cash register ring and glanced up to see the man in a blue uniform paying his bill.

"You staying open late tonight, Mister Barrett?" the man asked.

"Yep. Figure there'll be some customers after the big doings across the street."

"I'll be in for coffee afterward."

"You got death house duty again?"

"My name's on the list." The man in uniform pocketed his change and left.

Death house duty. Pearl winced at the words.

She stood and put on her coat and went to the counter.

"Ten cents, Miss," the man at the register said.

Pearl put two nickels on the counter. "Is there a return bus to Louisville late tonight—sometime after midnight, I mean?"

"Not until late tomorrow morning. There's a train though, one-thirty. It stops at Kuttawa, two miles down the road."

"Is there a hotel in town? Somewhere I could get a room for the afternoon?"

"Right down the hill, middle of town. Better hurry, though. Not many rooms, and lots of visitors expected tonight."

She nodded and left.

He watched her walk down the hill toward town. He'd been right about her, he concluded. She intended to spend the afternoon and evening in Eddyville, but wanted to leave as soon after midnight as possible.

She was there for a final farewell to one of the men taking their last walk that night.

10

The speakers across the hall blared a brassy rendition of "Stardust." Tom Penney listened for a few minutes, then mentally tuned out the distraction and read through the letter he had just finished.

How many letters had he written in the last—this final—year? he wondered. One a day, at least. Four hundred? Probably more. There had been letters to Father George, that gentle persuader whose indomitable passion for the Faith had convinced Tom that there was, indeed, divine absolution for the truly repentant; to Sister Robert Ann and Sister Laurentia, whose Christian concern had reached into "Murderers Row" to redeem a damned soul during its final months of earthly sojourn; to his mother, always in contrition, ever trying to ease her pain; and, least likely of all for a convicted murderer, to his ardent fans across the country who, captivated by broadcast and print stories about his penance and rebirth, were moved to commune through correspondence with this widely heralded penitent. His letters were always literate and finely composed, as letters written by earnest readers tend to be.

Now, as he read back over his final letter to his mother, the guilt of a lifetime, searing and inexpiable, tore at his guts. He thought he might vomit. But there was nothing on his stomach to come up, and slowly the nausea passed.

He envisioned his mother's anguished face, as he'd seen it every day as she sat in somber silence on the front row at his trial. He envisioned her as she had been during the tearful visits to his cell in the Lexington jail, where, on the day he was to be transported to the death house at Eddyville, she clung to him until guards had to pry her away. He had forbidden her to come here, to his final incarceration. He didn't want her remembering him in this morbid death house setting. For twenty-five years he had brought her little more than pain. Yet she had never renounced him, never recanted her love for him, never ceased in her prayerful attempts to sway him toward a better existence. She had collapsed on being told that he had confessed to the Miley slayings. Oh, how the press had jumped on that story! She had suffered the lurid tabloid accounts of his role in the murders. And tonight, he knew, in those harrowing minutes just after midnight, she would suffer vicariously his final atonement for the sins of an abhorrent life.

He studied the letter again. How inadequate it was. He had tried once more to explain the passion now rooted in his heart. Tried to convince her, as he had so often attempted to do in previous letters, that now that he had accepted the Faith, death held no fears for him. No, it was *living* that frightened him. He'd never done that well. For him, now, death was not an end but a beginning—a new and glorious beginning. He prayed that his final words to her would somehow ease the suffering his meaningless life had caused her, suffering he knew would continue until she herself was released by death.

He kissed the letter gently and placed it on the bed with the others. Then he reached above the bed and crossed off his mother's name for the last time.

He counted the sheets of paper he had left. Four—enough for the one letter still to be written, the all-important letter he would write during his final hour. He glanced across the corridor at the clock: 2:45 P.M. That final hour was approaching fast, he mused. But none too fast for him.

He pushed the letters aside and lay back on the bed. He was exhausted from hunger and lack of sleep, and his head throbbed. He had refused Captain Rankin's offer of aspirin. Let it throb. Let the pain mount. Let the poker-hot buzzsaw ripping his brain become his final—no, the next to final penance. Soon his pain would be cured forever.

A squeaky laugh came from the middle cell.

"Hey, Tom," Willie Baxter called, "you read Dick Tracy today?"

Tom pressed the heels of his hands hard against his temples. "No, Willie, I didn't."

"You oughta. It's good. He's after this bad guy whose been messin' with Junior." Willie chuckled again. "Boy, that Dick Tracy's sure something, he is."

God, what stupidity! Tom thought. No, make that innocence. Whatever, it was maddening. Nine hours left to live and Willie's profoundest thoughts were on the happenings in some inane comic strip.

He heard the paper plop onto the floor in Willie's cell. Willie's voice followed: "Guess I ain't gonna get to see how it comes out, tho'." Short pause. "Hey, Tom . . . can I ask you somethin'?"

"Sure."

"Is it . . . gonna hurt?"

Tom threw his legs over the side of the bed and stood. *God forgive me.* Willie *was* thinking about it. Tom pressed his face against the bars, sorry that he couldn't see Willie. "No, it won't hurt."

"Archie says some guys get burned real bad," Willie said. "He says he's smelled 'em. Says it stinks somethin' awful."

"Archie's full of shit, Willie. It won't be that way. It will be instantaneous. You'll be unconscious in a split second . . . you won't even know what hit you. And the next thing you see will be the greatest sight you've ever known."

There was further silence while Willie's mind worked this out. "You're talkin' about Heaven, ain't you?"

"Yes, I am."

"Yeah, well, all I know's what you and Brother Chandler been tellin' me. I sure hope you two're right."

"Look, Willie . . . you got somebody coming today? Pearl maybe?"

"No. Her an' me got nothin' goin' no more."

"A minister then? Have you asked for one?"

"Naw, I ain't asked for nobody. Brother Chandler said he'd be here tonight, though."

"Father Libs will be here, too. Would you pray with him, Willie?"

"I thought you and Libs was on the outs."

"We patched that up. Will you pray with him? I'd like for you to do that, Willie."

"Guess it won't hurt none."

"Good," Tom said. "I'll let him know just as soon as he gets here. You won't regret it."

You won't regret it.

No sooner had he spoken the words than they triggered an anguishing memory. He returned to his bed, his thoughts now on Willie. If guilt could be ranked, surely what he had done to that guileless little man who had trusted him would stand near the top of the list. When had it begun? He remembered that the day was hot. June? No . . . July. Just before the fourth, in that crucial summer before last . . .

Tom Penney was driving a delivery truck for Wiedemann Distributors that summer, hauling beer around Lexington and the suburbs. It was a tedious, stop-and-go operation. A case of Blue Ribbon here, two cases of Schlitz there. Unload, collect, write out a receipt, then on to the next customer and do the same again. It was sweltering, boring work, but it kept the parole officer off his back.

The weekly delivery to the Lexington Country Club was a welcome respite. Never just one or two cases there. Two dozen, mixed, was the minimum. And there was never any hassle about the bill. Moreover, after unloading, he always loafed for a half-hour or so beneath the mimosas down near the putting greens to watch the golfers practice. He didn't understand golf. Pool was his game.

Fourth of July that year fell on Friday. On Thursday, Tom arrived at the club with the largest order of the year—fifty cases, all bottles. The gentry were persnickety about beer in cans.

The huge colonial-style clubhouse sat atop a wooded hill remote from the fairways. The parking area was on the opposite side of the building from the storage coolers. It was a scorching afternoon, humid after a sudden shower, and the work was rigorous. Tom would enter the truck, move six cases to the rear door, jump to the ground, and load the cases onto a dolly, then wheel them around the hill on a rough cobblestone walkway to the walk-in cooler. He had unloaded and stacked the first dolly-load that day and was back inside the truck when he heard a high-pitched voice call out, "Need some help?"

He glanced around to see a puny, pinch-faced little man wearing a hopeful smile staring at him. Tom wiped the sweat from his eyes. "Sure could use some."

The small man rolled up his sleeves, jumped into the truck, and started shoving cases toward the rear. "I'm Ray Baxter. Most folks call me Willie. I keep up the greens here, do other odd jobs."

Tom jumped to the ground and started loading the cases onto the dolly. "Tom Penney. Glad to meet you, Willie. Listen . . . much obliged."

His puniness notwithstanding, Willie could work, and they had the truck unloaded and the cases stored in the cooler in half the normal time. Tom was grateful. Now he had even more time to loaf before the next delivery.

"What's your favorite beer, Willie?"

"Bud."

Tom entered the truck and brought out six bottles of Budweiser and handed them to Willie. Willie beamed as if he had been handed a sack of emeralds. "Hey . . . mighty white of you. Listen, I got some bottles iced down over at my shack. Wanna go splash down a few?"

Tom took a towel from the cab and dried his face and arms. "Best offer I've had all day."

Willie beamed anew. "C'mon."

The clapboard shack a quarter-mile downhill from the clubhouse consisted of a single large room with an adjoining bathroom. It had been converted from one end of a weather-beaten gardening shed. Inside was a steel cot shoved against one wall, a soiled overstuffed couch, a plain pine dinette table painted white, and a matching chair, all resting on a cement floor covered with cracked linoleum. Piles of dirty laundry, old newspapers, and comic books were strewn around the room. At one end of the sink counter, next to a two-burner electric hot plate, was a small oaken icebox.

"You live here?" Tom asked.

"Not alla time," Willie replied. "I got my own place a little ways down the road from the club. Mostly though I hang out here at the shack, after Mrs. Miley let me fix it up."

He took two bottles of beer from the box and uncapped them at an opener screwed into the wall. When he handed one of the beers to his guest, Tom noticed fresh puncture marks on the inside crook of Willie's arm. He looked closer and saw that Willie's eyes were dilated. The greenskeeper was a junkie.

Tom raised his beer. "Cheers."

"Mud in your eye," Willie replied.

Tom drained half the bottle in one gulp.

There was a plate of cold fried chicken on the table. Willie shoved it toward Tom.

Tom took a drumstick. "You cook this?"

"Naw. Mrs. Miley made it. She's my boss. She's one okay lady, she is . . . brings me somethin' most ever'day. Eat all you want."

Tom took a bite and gestured across the room. "What's with the birds?"

Two canaries were chirping merrily in a cage near an open jalousie window. Willie went to the cage, walking with the same wary gait he'd used at the truck, as if he was ever ready to spring away from some lurking danger. He checked the water dish, adjusted the whalebone clipped to the side, and made sure there was food in the cup.

"I like birds," he said, with feeling. "They're sorta like friends, you know. They keep me company." He pursed his lips and began to whistle and talk to the canaries as if they were children.

Tom watched it all with fascination. He wondered how many real friends this sad-looking little man had.

Willie came back to the table. "You got any pets, Tom? Any hobbies?"

"No . . . no pets. I like to read."

"Read? Read what?"

"Books."

"You mean . . . whole books?"

"Sure."

"Geez," Willie exclaimed. "I don't read none too good myself. Just the funny papers . . . and comic books. Never read a real book. How'd you learn that?"

"In stir," Tom replied.

"Stir?" Willie's voice raised a pitch. "Hey . . . where? What'd you do?"

"Frankfort," Tom replied. "Seven years. Armed robbery." He didn't reveal that he had shot two men while committing the crime.

It had the effect Tom expected. Willie slapped his leg in glee. "Hot damn! Stir! That's sure something, that is." Then a glimpse of suspicion crossed his face. "How come you're driving a beer truck now? You ain't bullshittin' me, are you?"

Despite an instinct that told him he could trust Willie, Tom wasn't ready to put his intuition to the test. He didn't explain that his delivery job made him privy to whiskey shipments throughout Central Kentucky; that he selected certain late-arriving trucks for robbing; that he forced entry into warehouses and stole the cargo before the trucks were scheduled to be off-loaded the next day; that he was in cahoots with a nightclub owner in Louisville who bought all the illegal booze he could deliver.

Instead, Tom said, "The job came with the parole. It keeps the parole officer off my ass."

"Yeah . . . I guess that's right," Willie said.

Tom said, "How about you?"

Willie looked puzzled. "Huh?"

Tom tapped Willie on the inside of his arm. "Those aren't mosquito bites. And you don't support a habit like that mowing the greens around a golf course. What's the scam?"

Willie blanched and rolled his sleeves down. "You're one smart man, you are. You wouldn't put the finger on me, would ya?"

"Ah, shit, man . . . give me a break."

Willie emitted a nervous laugh. "Well, yeah, I make a little on the side."

He glanced around nervously, then lowered his voice. "The guys who play here . . . real gents, you know . . . well-heeled, some of 'em, anyway. They like their kicks, know what I mean? I got me a contact up in Covington, brings me down a few sticks ever' now and then . . ."

"A few?"

"Well, couple a' hundred, maybe. I get a cut rate, see. And I get a pretty good mark up here. Two bucks a stick. It's all on the Q.T., hear? Mrs. Miley found out, she'd can my ass proper. Don't hurt no one though . . . honest."

He looked at Tom, beseeching understanding.

So Willie peddled reefers to the social elite. Tom smiled. "Sure. No harm done. Good for the old farts, really. Helps them keep it up."

Willie slapped his leg again. "Hey! Never thought of that. That's rich that is."

They both laughed.

The following Thursday when Willie again volunteered to help unload the beer truck—it would become a weekly routine—Tom asked how the Fourth of July dance had turned out.

"Best ever," Willie responded. "Eighteen grand."

Tom sputtered. "Eighteen . . . you mean eighteen thousand dollars?!"

"That's what Mrs. Miley said."

Tom emitted a low whistle.

One day in August Willie asked Tom if he'd like to meet his girlfriend. "Name's Lola LaRue . . . you know, the actress." He gave Tom an expectant look.

"Lola LaRue?"

"Well, her real name's Pearl . . . Pearl Smith. She's got a carny act now—Rape of the Maiden. Out near UK. You gotta catch it. Pearl's some classy dame."

Rape of the Maiden? That he had to see, Tom decided. "When? How'll we get there?"

"How 'bout tomorrow night? Mrs. Miley lets me use the pickup. Maybe we'll run out to the Trocodero later, make a night of it."

Tom agreed. He wanted to talk to Willie about a business proposition anyway, one he'd been mulling ever since he learned about the take from the Fourth of July dance.

The carnival was one of those ramshackle shows that traveled the South playing college towns. It had been set up near the University of Kentucky campus all summer. There was a creaking Ferris wheel, a carrousel with half the mounts broken, a "death defying" loop-the-loop that appeared true to its billing, and, the main enticement for the college crowd, an assortment of sleazy side shows. Every week the manager distributed discount coupons to the nearby fraternity houses, and most of the gawkers each night were students.

Willie led Tom past a row of side shows: "Night in a Harem," "The Farmer's Daughter," "Turkish Delights." At the last tent the marquee proclaimed:

ON STAGE IN PERSON
Miss Lola LaRue
In Her Sensational Pantomime
RAPE OF THE MAIDEN

Willie pointed with pride. "This is it. C'mon." He plunked down fifty cents for two tickets and led Tom through the tent flap.

Inside, a dozen backless wooden benches sat amid sprinkled sawdust, discarded popcorn boxes, candy wrappers, and other accumulated litter. A single low-wattage bulb dangled from the center pole. Another hung above the stage, where backdrops were painted to resemble a bedroom. There was a tarnished brass bed covered with a multi-colored quilt at center stage.

Willie urged Tom toward the front bench. Tom noticed that the audience was all male, all young.

The audience light switched off. From backstage came the sound of a needle trying to find the groove on a scratchy record. After a moment the tent was filled with a tinny refrain from "Night and Day."

A lone figure entered from stage-right. Willie nudged Tom. "That's her . . . that's Pearl."

The woman's left side, facing the audience, was made up as a young girl: blonde wig, short-sleeve sweater, yellow plaid skirt, bobby socks, saddle shoes. Her left cheek and eye were gaudily highlighted with rouge and eye shadow to portray wide-eyed innocence.

There was a rap at the fake door. Pearl cupped her left hand to her ear. "Hark!"

The audience guffawed.

Pearl crossed the stage with an exaggerated sway, keeping the single light between her and the audience so that her right side remained in shadow. She made a gesture of opening the door, then recoiled in mock horror. Instantly, she whirled to present her right side to the audience. From this angle her costume was male: black trousers leg, long-sleeve sweater, pull-over knit cap.

Her facial make-up was swarthy, presenting the appearance of a rogue.

The audience hissed and booed the villain.

Willie whistled and stomped his feet.

Tom thought it was the worst act he'd ever seen.

On stage, Pearl began a pirouetting struggle between good and evil, rogue advancing and maiden retreating, each whirl moving the action closer to center stage. When she reached the bed she fell back on it, maiden side to the audience. The black-sleeved arm of the rogue threw itself across her body, the hand worked it way beneath the sweater and manipulated the maiden's breast. Then it grasped the skirt roughly and raised it waist high. The bare left leg arched, the black-trousered leg and meandering arm twisted about to give the appearance of the rogue assuming a position atop the maiden. Pearl contorted her body with fervor.

The music changed to bump and grind. The rogue thrust, the maiden recoiled, the audience grunted in unison, all to the burlesque beat. The music quickened, grew louder, hit crescendo. Climax! Pearl's entwined bodies quivered, collapsed in spent passion, and lay still. The stage went dark.

The audience howled, stomped, and whistled.

Willie led the accolade. "What'd I tell you, Tom." He was clapping so hard that it hurt Tom's ears. "That was somethin', huh?"

"Yeah, Willie. That sure was something, all right."

"C'mon," Willie said, "I'll get us a couple of more tickets. She's only got one more show, then we can go to the Troc."

Tom gave an inward moan, but acquiesced. He had important things to discuss with Willie tonight, and he'd just have to suffer through the prelude.

The crowd at the Trocodero was sparse. Willie and Tom ordered a pitcher of bock beer and two glasses. When Pearl ordered a Tom Collins, Willie winked at Tom. "Didn't I tell you? Real class."

Tom studied the pair. Willie was holding Pearl's hand and staring at her like a lap dog in heat. More guarded, Pearl catered to Willie while frequently glancing at Tom with that same haunted look of an animal at bay that characterized her boyfriend. She looked much older than Willie, older than himself for that matter. But with someone like that it was difficult to judge. She may have been pretty once. She was thin to the point of gauntness. Her deep-set, rueful eyes had the burned-out look of one who had seen too much too soon. Once, when she turned toward Willie, Tom spotted a grotesque feature beneath her wispy dark hair. Her right ear had been severed at the base, as if removed in one determined slash of a razor. Tom recognized the tell-tale mark for what it was. Along the Ohio Riverfront towns it was the brand of a whore who had tried to hold out on her pimp.

A western-attired trio was playing over-amplified corn pone music. Willie and Pearl danced. Willie invited Tom to dance with Pearl, but Tom declined, pleading two left feet. He chain-smoked Chesterfields and swilled glass after glass of beer, biding his time, waiting to get a few minutes alone with Willie.

At the next intermission, Pearl excused herself to go to the powder room.

"Nice," Tom said as she walked away.

"Yeah," Willie agreed. "We hit it off real good. You got a butt, Tom?"

The nearby tables were empty. Tom shook a Chesterfield loose and held the pack out to Willie. Then he held a match while Willie lit up. "Listen"—Tom kept his voice low—"about that eighteen grand your boss lady took in . . . is it like that always?"

"Naw . . . that was special. Most times it's twelve . . . fifteen grand."

"Every weekend? Cold cash?"

"Yeah. More when they hold a big bash of some kind."

"What's the old lady do with it? Over the weekend, I mean . . . take it to a night deposit somewhere?"

"Uh-uh. She keeps it in her office downstairs. She's got a cash box in her desk."

Tom mulled it over. "You mean that every Friday and

Saturday night there's twelve to fifteen thousand dollars stashed in an unguarded cash box downstairs in that big clubhouse, and only one old woman asleep upstairs?"

Slow to comprehend, Willie nonetheless grasped the motive behind Tom's question. He frowned. "Aw . . . come off it, Tom. Mrs. Miley's the only one ever treated me halfway decent, 'cept Pearl and you. I ain't gonna do nothin' to hurt her. You ain't either."

There was a firmness in Willie's voice that Tom hadn't bargained for. "Hey . . . come on, Willie. What do you take me for? I don't mean any harm to the old lady. Hell, she'd never even know I was in the place. Besides, it's no skin off her nose. That kind of money is pocket change to the fat cats she caters to. Shit, man, they could make that up in one damned hoe-down."

He leaned closer. "Look, all I need is a lookout, someone to make sure that no one surprises me. I can do the rest by myself. Christ, it'd be like picking money up off the street. What do you say?"

Willie shook his head. The conversation was visibly upsetting him. "No . . . no. I couldn't rob her. No way."

Tom sensed he was losing ground. He moderated his tone. "Okay, Willie. I guess you couldn't. No problem. Look, I can recruit another person to help. There's plenty for a three-way split. You wouldn't even have to be there. All you'd have to do is meet me down by the gate with a key to the clubhouse, or else just make sure the downstairs door's unlocked that night. No noise that way, see? In and out. Quick and clean. And think of this . . . with your cut you could sure do something real nice for Pearl."

"Yeah . . . but . . ."

The little man was wavering. Tom saw Pearl crossing the dance floor. Not enough time to press further. "I understand, Willie. Just think it over, all right? And"—he put a finger to his lips—"mum's the word."

Willie nodded.

It went that way for weeks. Casual. No pressure. On delivery days Tom would mention the heist in an off-hand way, subtly replaying the theme of what Willie could do for Pearl with his share. Wisely, he didn't force the issue.

Until late one evening in September.

It was almost midnight when Willie heard a car screech to a halt in front of his shack. He jumped out of bed and opened the door to see Tom jump down from the cab of the beer truck. Tom stalked into the shack in a rage.

"Jesus, Tom . . . what's wrong?"

Tom was shaking with anger. "That asshole saloon keeper in Louisville, the guy I told you about . . . Anderson. He's really stuck it to me, Willie, that's what's wrong. I've been hijacking booze for him ever since I got out of stir. Premium stuff . . . bonded. Tonight I took him a load of scotch. Son of a bitch said it was green. Accused me of trying to rip him off. Green my ass! It's me whose getting ripped off. He offered to take it off my hands for a fourth of the usual price—real gentleman-like."

Willie got a couple of beers from the icebox and handed one to Tom. Tom took a swig and slammed the bottle down hard on the table. "I'll get that chiseling bastard if it's the last thing I ever do."

Willie had never seen Tom so agitated. He said nothing.

Tom killed the beer in another swig. "Willie, I'm in a real jam. I was counting on the payoff from that load of hootch. Now I've got to come up with a bundle real fast. Look, I haven't pressed you about the club heist, you know that. But things have changed. I've been playing the nags out at Barney's . . . "

Barney's was a bookie joint located in south Lexington. It was one of a score or more of betting parlors operating in the tri-state area of Kentucky, Indiana, and Ohio by an eastern cartel.

" . . . I'm in over my head. Unless I can come up with some hard cash soon I'm gonna be wading the bottom of the Ohio with cement boots."

"Geez . . . geez . . . ," Willie sputtered.

Tom fixed the little man with an imploring look. "You're the only one who can help me now, Willie. It all depends on whether you're a true friend or not. If not, just say the word and I'll get the hell out of your life forever. But if you are . . . if us being pals means anything to you . . . then it's time to shit or get off the pot. There's a big shindig coming off out here Friday night. It's in all the papers. It'll be the perfect night. Hit and run. No muss, no fuss. What do you say?"

Willie's voice quavered. "Hell, Tom . . . you know I'm your friend."

"Then act like it, damn it!"

Tom's tone made Willie flinch. "All . . . all I gotta do's leave the door unlocked? You won't hurt Mrs. Miley none?"

"Not a hair on her head. You got my word on that, Willie."

His countenance reflecting his quandary, Willie nodded. "I . . . guess so."

Tom reached over and slapped his tormented pal on the shoulder. "Attaboy, Willie. I knew you wouldn't let me down. Look, it'll be okay. You won't regret it. I promise you that."

"You won't regret it . . . ever."

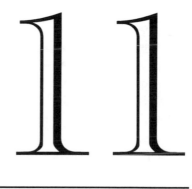

Robert Anderson paced the floor of his cell fitfully—bed to wall, door to window—pausing on occasion to peer out between the bars at the world beyond his reach. From time to time he glanced at the clock across the hallway. *Where the hell are my lawyers? One of them should have called by now.*

The last hour had been enough to drive any sane man crazy. First there'd been that idiotic exchange between Willie and Tom.

Will it hurt?

Father Libs will pray for you.

Penney and Baxter. Asshole and nitwit. It was enough to make a grown man puke.

Then there had been that maddening business with Captain Rankin. The old man had come to the cells, pen and pad in hand, to take orders for the last meal. *The last meal!* Tom and Willie had given their orders—steak, fried chicken, mashed potatoes, peas, lettuce and tomato salad, biscuits, butter, cigars—as painstakingly as if they'd been dining in Leo's Hideaway in Louisville. Captain Rankin had laughed at Willie's playful order for a case of Budweiser. "Off limits, son . . . sorry."

When the captain asked Bob for his order, Bob blew a gasket. "There's not going to be any goddamned last meal for me today, damnit! Feed your slop to those two pigs who ordered it."

Captain Rankin had shrugged. "There'll be enough for all."

Frustration mounting, Bob sat on the edge of his bed and rubbed a clenched fist hard into his palm. Where in the hell were his lawyers?!

They had explained things so neatly during their last visit. In the face of the uncertainty Tom Penney had stirred up, no governor would have the guts to let Anderson burn. Tom's refusal to testify further wasn't an insurmountable problem. A lot of people were digging into Buford Stewart's past, particularly on the night of the murders. That could prove dangerous to any astute politician. Governor Johnson was no fool. He might let it go down to the wire, just to see if Anderson cracked. But a stay of execution was as certain as sunrise tomorrow.

Well, Bob thought, if Johnson doesn't act soon, there'll be no sunrise tomorrow.

He looked again at the clock. It was 3:01 P.M. The lawyers were scheduled to meet with the governor at 10:00. Give an hour or so for unforseen circumstances, it should all have been settled by noon. A stay of execution. How long should it take to plead a cut-and-dried mitigation anyway?

Where in the hell had everybody been for the past three hours?

How long did it take to make one damned phone call?

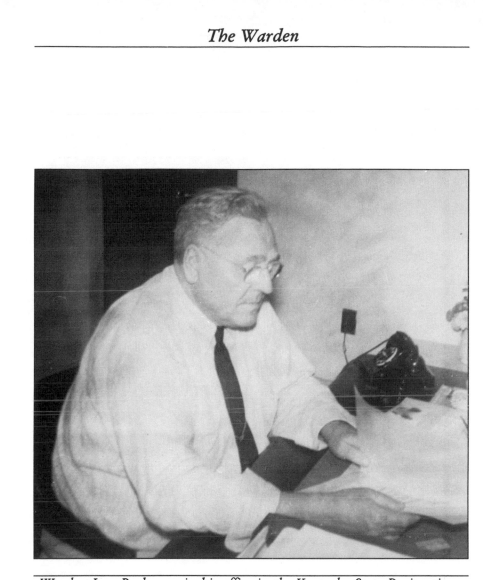

Warden Jesse Buchanan in his office in the Kentucky State Penitentiary, circa 1940. (photo: Kentucky State Penitentiary)

The Kentucky State Penitentiary as it was at the time of the Miley case. The Cumberland River runs in the foreground. At far right, at the top of the slope, stands the private home of the elderly Mr. & Mrs. Catlett. (photo: Lyon County Historical Society)

The front steps of Kentucky State Penitentiary, scene of the fatal shoot-out involving prison escapees Robert McNair and Earl Gibbs. (photo: Lyon County Historical Society)

Warden Buchanan's Chief of Staff, Porter Lady, who faced down the escaping convicts. (photo: Porter Lady, Jr.)

Golf champion Marion Miley, 27, and her mother, Elsie, 52, director of the Lexington Country Club. (photos: Lexington Country Club.)

The Crime

Amid news of the war in Europe, the Miley murder case as it was reported on the front page of the New York Times, September 29, 1941.

(photos: The Courier-Journal)

Top left: Lexington Country Club greenskeeper Raymond "Willie" Baxter, age 27, at the time of his arrest.

Above: Robert Anderson, the 37-year-old nightclub owner who protested his innocence, flanked by Lexington detectives.

Left: Tom Penney, 33, being returned to Kentucky following his Texas capture.

The Trial

The convicted murderers returning to Lexington for Robert Anderson's final hearing for a new trial. From left to right, front row: Warden Buchanan, Willie Baxter, Tom Penney; back row: State Police Capt. Noel Jones, Robert Anderson. At far right is young William Buchanan—the author—age seventeen. (photo: The Courier-Journal)

12

"Willie!"

No response.

"*Willie* . . . wake up!"

She shook him by the shoulder and turned on the light. He shaded his eyes. "What's goin' on, Pearl?"

"I heard shots."

"Shots?" He rubbed his eyes.

"Up on the hill. I know what guns sound like. Somebody's shooting up at the clubhouse."

Shots?

Shots!

Willie sat bolt upright. *Oh, Jesus!* He was supposed to have left the clubhouse door unlocked tonight. *I forgot!*

He jumped out of bed and pulled his trousers on over his nakedness.

Shots. No! Tom promised.

Pearl pulled the blanket around her shoulders. "Should we call the police?"

"Huh? No! No cops . . . not yet."

He fumbled with a button on his shirt. "I'm gonna go up and take a look."

He ran out of the shack in his bare feet, started the pickup after a couple of fumbling tries and roared away up the hill. He stopped in the parking lot in front of the clubhouse and let the truck lights play on the building. The front door, standing wide open, looked damaged. He glanced around the parking lot, then down the main driveway. A car light briefly illuminated the entry gate. Had the car just left the grounds? He couldn't tell. There was no one in sight, no sound other than the eerie silence of the dark autumn night. For a long while he sat there motionless, trying to sort it all out.

Pearl was wrong, he bet. She didn't know nothing about guns. What'd happened was that Tom had jimmied the door, grabbed the cash box, and drove off in a hurry, backfiring his car engine. That was it. That's what Pearl heard. Backfire. Not shots. He wheeled the truck around. He'd better get back to the shack and set Pearl straight. He'd have to make up some story. Mrs. Miley would find the money missing tomorrow and call the cops. He'd just keep out of it.

He started back toward the shack. Halfway there, he turned around and left the grounds and drove to a local bar where he'd spent the earlier part of that night drinking with Tom. Maybe Tom had gone back there, and would tell him what had happened. But the bar was closed. He wondered if he should go to Tom's house, but decided that would be too risky. Confused, wondering what to do next, he drove around the dark streets of Lexington in a daze. After what seemed an eternity, he drove back to the country club and stopped again in front of the clubhouse.

Perhaps it wouldn't hurt none to take a quick gander inside. Just to make sure Tom hadn't left something behind to trip them up. Just don't touch nothing.

He took a flashlight from the glove compartment. Then, leaving the truck engine running, he got out and walked through the open door into the clubhouse. . . .

Willie Baxter sat staring at the floor of his cell, his mind riveted on the horror he had found on the other side of that open door that night long ago when Pearl shook him awake. The night he discovered "the God-awful thing I did."

The "God-awful thing" that occurred that tragic September night came at a time when Willie's aimless life was at last beginning to take order. He had found a place where he felt wanted. He had a permanent job and a good boss. Then, in the course of one fateful summer, he found a good friend and a good woman.

Fact was, he met Pearl before he met Tom.

It happened the evening Mrs. Miley brought him the stew. He had been pruning evergreens along the back fairways and finished late. He came back to his shack, drank a couple of beers, then took down a can of Campbell's Pork and Beans from the cupboard for supper. He liked Campbell's Pork and Beans. Bigger chunks of pork than in the other brands. And there was no fuss, no muss. Just open them up, dump them onto a piece of wax paper, and scoop them into your mouth with crackers. No plates or forks to wash.

He had just grabbed the can opener when there was a knock at the door. When he opened it, Mrs. Miley rushed inside. "Stand aside . . . this is hot."

She hurried across the room and set a large bowl of stew, chunky with beef and vegetables, on the table. "I saw you working late and knew you wouldn't take time to fix yourself a decent dinner."

Willie was genuinely pleased. "Thank you, ma'am. I still got some of that pecan pie. Sure is good."

"I'm glad you like my cooking, Willie."

She studied him for a long moment. During his first months at the country club, right after she had hired him, he had been so painfully shy and evasive that it was impossible to carry on a decent conversation with him. He would take orders, and he worked hard. But his countenance remained that of a whipped dog. His wretchedness tore at her heart, and with firm resolve she set about to bring whatever sunshine she could into his life. She passed up no opportunity to praise his work, to see to it that he ate well, that his quarters on the grounds were comfortable. In time, her compassion paid dividends. He was beginning to spend more time here in the shack she let him occupy than in the room he had in town. No longer did he stare at the ground when they were talking. Better yet, he had begun to smile, to be more open with her. But there was still a long way to go.

"Willie," she said that day she brought the stew, "I don't mean to pry into your private life, but I notice you don't go out evenings. It's not good for a young person like yourself to stay cooped up all the time. Don't you have any friends you could go visit? Or invite to visit you here? I wouldn't mind."

Willie shook his head. "I don't go out much. Just a movie sometimes." He perked up and nodded across the room. "I got my birds, though."

Mrs. Miley was a thick-set woman, taller than he, with short hair and kindly eyes behind gold-rimmed glasses. When she spoke again it was like a mother admonishing her child.

"Birds are no substitute for people, Willie. You need friends, someone your own age to talk to, to let off steam with, to confide in. Now, I want you to quit sitting around this shack every night. I want you to go out, meet people. Find yourself a nice girl. There'll be plenty of time to vegetate when you get old. I understand there's a carnival playing over near the university. Why don't you go? Would you like an advance on next week's pay?"

"No ma'am. I got money."

"Then there's no excuse not to go. Take the truck. It'll do you good."

So, like an obedient son, he went.

He strolled among the crowded booths, pitched pennies, threw a baseball at stacked milk bottles, tried to guess the number of beans in a gallon jug. He spent money, won nothing, and didn't enjoy himself. He'd rather have been home reading his comic books. At last, deciding that his commitment to Mrs. Miley had been fulfilled, he started to leave.

He had parked the truck on a side street reached by a path that took him past a row of sideshows. At the last tent a marquee caught his eye:

ON STAGE IN PERSON
Miss Lola LaRue
In Her Sensational Pantomime
<u>RAPE OF THE MAIDEN</u>

A sign said the entrance fee was twenty-five cents.

It was still early. He went to the booth and pushed a quarter through the window. A fat man tore a ticket in half and told Willie to go inside.

As he always did when he went to the movies, he took a seat in the front row. The audience was mostly young men who hooted, stomped, roared, and hissed at Lola LaRue's outrageous act.

Willie was enthralled. It was the first time he'd ever seen a live stage act, and it moved him as no Saturday matinee ever had. Enchanted as he was with the act, he was even more enthralled with the actress. A real live actress, with ability to play on his emotions, to remove him temporarily from the drab reality of his life, to cause him to care about *her* plight.

When the audience filed out, Willie sat motionless, staring at the empty stage. Minutes later a stagehand wearing outsize overalls appeared and started to make the rumpled bed. Spotting Willie, the stagehand barked, "Hey, buster, out! Show's over."

It was a feminine voice. Willie squeaked, "Miss LaRue?"

"Yeah."

"You were good. Real good."

"Thanks. Now get outa here. I've gotta set up for the next show. You wanna stay you'll have to buy another ticket."

With uncharacteristic boldness Willie persisted. "Hey . . .

you know what? You oughta be in the movies."

She emitted a caustic laugh. "Sure I should. And you just happen to know a guy who knows a guy who can get me a date for a screen test. Bullshit, buster. Shove off. I'm running late as it is."

Willie stood up and shoved his hands deep into his pants pocket. "Naw . . . I don't know nobody like that. Well . . . so long."

He had reached the canvas doorway when she called out, "Hey you! Wait up."

She hiked up the ill-fitting overalls, jumped down from the stage, and walked up the trash-strewn aisle to where he stood. She looked him over, curious. "Look, mister"—her voice was softer now—"are you for real?"

She was still in heavy makeup and he couldn't see her true features. He stared, puzzled. "Uh . . . real?"

"Did you mean what you said back there, about liking my act and all?"

"Yes ma'am. It was real good."

"Well, I'll be damned. That's right sweet of you, Mister . . . Mister . . . ?"

"Naw . . . not Mister. Just Ray . . . Ray Baxter. Most folks call me Willie."

"Willie, huh? Well, look Willie, I got a couple more shows to do tonight. Why don't you stick around? My guest. Afterwards we can go someplace and get a drink. That is, if you want to."

He could hardly believe this turn of good fortune. "Hey! That'd be great, Miss La Rue."

"See you later, then."

She started to go, then turned and smiled through the greasepaint. "And my real name's Pearl . . . Pearl Smith."

And so their relationship began.

Every night after work, with Mrs. Miley's blessing, Willie borrowed the truck and drove to the carnival in time to catch Pearl's last act. Afterward, they'd get a hamburger or a bowl of chili at the carny mess tent, then drive around town, sometimes talking away the hours until dawn. Whatever good looks Pearl might have once possessed had long before faded behind a mask of cynicism. Yet, from the start she sensed that she was more to Willie than just a carny-lot pick up. She had filled a void in his life. More surprising, she realized that he had done the same in hers.

On Saturday nights they would drive out to the Trocodero. The nightclub on Route 60 near Keeneland Race Track was noted for authentic Italian food and a different country-western band every month. Indifferent to food, Willie and Pearl had a few drinks and concentrated on the down-home music and each other. Willie had never danced before. Pearl taught him the two-step and the square, and after a few lessons he was able to stumble through the slow pieces without constantly looking at his feet. He refused to jitterbug.

It was at the Trocodero, the second week after they met, that Pearl said, "Willie, you're fighting the monkey, aren't you?"

He reacted like a little boy who'd been caught in a naughty act. "I was gonna tell you."

She put a hand on his. "Come on now, don't cloud up. Hell, I'm no angel myself, you know. I just wanted to know for sure. How big?"

"Twenty bucks a day."

Six hundred dollars a month!

"How do you handle that, honey?" she asked.

He confided in her about the reefer trade at the club. "I got some customers, well-heeled, you know? Some of 'em . . . dames, too . . . take five, ten sticks every weekend. It's good for a couple a hundred a week. I got no expenses 'cept my room in town. And I don't use that much anymore, what with the shack and all."

"You just sell reefers . . . nothing else?"

"No, nothin' else . . . honest, Pearl."

She was relieved. She'd known junkies all her life and knew how most of them supported their habits: burglaries, muggings, armed robberies, pimping, sometimes worse. In one way or another she had been touched by them all. She wondered if Willie had done any of those things before hitting on the country club scam. Dope was a cruel master. She decided not to pursue that angle of the past, yet.

"Have you ever tried to kick it, honey?"

"Yeah. Cold turkey. Like to of killed me."

"Some people do it, you know."

He didn't respond.

"Look, if you ever need help . . . I mean, if you ever want to try again, I'm here. Okay?"

He was distressed by this turn in the conversation, but at the same time deeply touched. Pearl *cared*. No one else ever had—except Mrs. Miley. He dreaded the thought that someday that kind old lady might find out that he was a junkie, or worse, that he was peddling dope on the country club grounds. For reasons he couldn't explain, or even understand, he valued Mrs. Miley's good opinion of him. As for the rest of them, Willie Baxter could drop in the gutter and drown on his own puke for all they cared. Tough titty. Good riddance. But now, someone else cared, too.

He finally managed to stammer, "Jesus, Pearl . . . I don't know. I . . . "

She sensed that his bewilderment was causing him to withdraw into himself.

"Okay, Willie. It's all right. Come on, let's dance."

That night, for the first time, she went with him to his shack.

His attempt at lovemaking, like his dancing, was awkward. Once again she became his teacher, showing him how to pace his fervor, to take it easy.

When he awoke next morning the floor had been swept, his comic books were stacked beside the bed, his clothes were neatly hung in the closet, the dishes were washed, the canaries had been fed, and the rich aroma of perking coffee came from the stove. Pearl was setting the table, in the nude.

He sat up. "I think I done died and gone to Heaven."

She smiled. "Thanks. But I told you . . . I'm no angel."

He beckoned her back to the bed. For the rest of the morning, before and after breakfast, they practiced what she had taught him the night before.

It was also that morning in bed that he asked her, "Pearl, how'd you lose your ear?"

"Couple of guys sliced it off."

"Jesus! How come?"

She didn't dissemble. "I was a hooker, Willie. It's a long story, and not a very pretty one. I'll tell you all about it someday. But not now. Let's not spoil things, okay?."

He thought about it. "Sure, okay. But, do you . . . uh . . . are you . . . ?"

"Still a whore?" She laughed. "No way. I get along fine at the carny. Don't have to screw anybody to keep the job. Don't have to screw anybody, period."

"You do me."

"Yeah. But I don't *have* to."

That afternoon as he drove her back to the carny lot he told her that he loved her. She'd already sensed it. More surprising, she sensed that she felt the same way about him. "You know, Willie," she said, "I never believed I'd ever say this to a man, but I love you, too."

She leaned over and kissed him on the cheek.

In August, Willie told Pearl that he was bringing a friend to see her act. He'd been talking about Tom Penney for days. "We'll drive out to the Trocodero after the last show. Tom's one okay guy. You're gonna like him a lot."

She didn't.

That night at the Trocodero she resented the cold-eyed way Tom kept sizing her up, as if she was a brood mare up for auction. Once, from the corner of her eye she caught the smirk that crossed his face when he spotted her ear had been severed. There was no mistaking that look. He knew what it meant: that she'd been a whore, and a trouble-making one at that. Then there was Tom's thinly concealed eagerness to be alone with Willie, obviously to speak of something he didn't want her to hear.

It was all over Willie's head. He had no grasp for subtlety. In his eyes they were all having a ball.

At the bandstand a "cowboy" singer closed a song on a

lingering high note. Tom sneered. "Punk. I hate a guy that sings like a woman."

Willie imitated the sneer. "Yeah . . . punk!"

To Pearl, it was a disgusting bootlicking reaction. Willie had no feeling one way or the other about the singer. He was currying favor with Tom.

She grabbed her purse and got up. "Back in a minute."

Willie stood. Tom didn't.

She did a low burn in the ladies room for fifteen minutes. If Tom Penney couldn't spit out whatever was stuck in his craw in that time, let him choke on it.

When she got back to the table, Willie's mood had changed. He strained at gaiety, but whatever had transpired between the two of them while she was gone had left him in a funk. Annoyed with the whole evening, she rose again and suggested they leave. No one argued.

They dropped Tom at his south-side rooming house then drove back across town to Willie's shack in silence. Once inside, Pearl threw her purse on the bed in anger.

"Willie, I don't like your friend Tom Penney one damned bit."

"Aw, Pearl . . . Tom's okay. This just wasn't his night."

"Okay my ass. I know all about messed-up bastards like him—ex-cons, losers, always trying to work an angle at someone else's expense. He's trouble, Willie, with a capital fucking T."

Willie shuffled nervously and studied a spot on his shoe. "Naw, Pearl, you got him all wrong. Tom ain't like that. Me and him are pals . . . a few beers ever' now and then . . . some laughs. Nothing else. Honest."

"Yeah? What did he say back there at the Troc to get you so down in the mouth?"

"Just some horseshit he's gettin' on the job," Willie lied. "That's all. He'll come 'round, though. Then you two'll hit it off real good. You'll see."

Icy silence. Finally, she said, "Willie, you are one dumb-ass jerk."

She undressed and climbed into the bed and turned her back

to him. He took off his clothes and climbed in beside her, his mind in turmoil. It was their first fight. He wondered if he should tell her what had happened at the Trocodero. The more he debated it in his mind the more confusing it became. It was no use. There was no way to explain to her that his best friend had just asked him to help rob the kindest lady he'd ever known.

Nor did he confide in Pearl a few weeks later when Tom came to the shack in a rage over the botched liquor deal with the Louisville nightclub owner, Bob Anderson. Or tell her that at Tom's pleading he had agreed to leave the clubhouse door open after the dance the following Saturday night.

By the time that fateful weekend rolled around, Pearl had put her spat with Willie out of mind. But, still rankled from that night at the Trocodero, she made her position clear. She never wanted to see the scar-faced ex-con again. If Willie wanted to continue his association with Tom Penney, that was his business. But he'd have to do it on his own, away from her. Far away.

For his part, Willie learned that the less said to Pearl about Tom, the better. Although tempted, he never confided in her about the planned robbery, or told her that his only reason for getting involved was for what he could do for her with his share of the loot.

And so it went, until that pre-dawn Sunday morning when Pearl heard gunfire.

In the earlier part of that evening, Willie had left Pearl at the shack and gone out alone. He'd come home late, long after she had gone to bed. He didn't dare tell her where he'd been, that he'd been drinking beer at a local bar with Tom Penny until well after midnight, that he'd promised to unlock the clubhouse door when he went home.

This night, he mused, as he parked for the second time in front of the clubhouse and walked toward that battered front door, flashlight in hand. And he'd forgotten to keep his one simple part of the bargain.

Willie's first thought on entering the clubhouse that morning was to check the office to see if the cash box was missing. Barefoot, he walked softly across the thick rug so as not to awaken Mrs. Miley upstairs. The office door was open. He shined the flashlight on the desk. The drawers and their contents lay scattered on the floor. The cash box lay in the far corner, open and empty. *Tom had succeeded.*

But why all the mess? Why had he left the cash box behind? Willie wondered if he should wipe things off. Then it came to him. *Gloves.* There wouldn't be any fingerprints because Tom would have been wearing gloves.

Relieved, he tiptoed back toward the front door. Halfway there he turned his light onto something out of place. He leaned down and held the light closer. *Blood?*

Had Tom cut himself opening the cash box? But there was no blood in the office. He shined the beam in a slow arc around the foyer. Then he saw it. A bloody trail leading across the large room and up the stairs toward Mrs. Miley's apartment.

A cold tremor shot up his spine. Did he dare go up those stairs? He wanted to flee, to leave whatever was at the top of that blackened stairway for others to find. Instead, driven by a compelling force, he crossed the foyer and climbed the steps, taking care not to leave a telling footprint in the blood.

At the top of the landing he shined the light toward Mrs. Miley's apartment. The door had been broken from its hinges. The flashlight in his hand began to quaver. He stepped across the threshold into the apartment. It was a shambles. The walls, rug, even the ceiling were blood-splattered and . . . could it be? He stooped low for a closer look. *Brains!*

Something took form in his peripheral vision. He swung the light quickly and froze. Lying on the hallway floor beside him, close enough for him to touch, was the body of a woman. Dressed in pajamas, she lay face down in a crumpled heap. Her head was split open and half her skull dangled to one side, held only by a few strands of gore-matted hair.

Willie gasped. "Mrs. Miley!"

In that moment of sheer terror Willie Baxter did not know that the defiled body he was looking at was not that of Mrs. Elsie Miley, but that of twenty-seven-year-old Marion Miley, home between golf tournaments for a visit with her mother. Nor did he know that the woman he thought he was looking at, whose bloody trail he had followed up the staircase, was at that moment crawling across the country club grounds with three bullet wounds in her stomach, in a desperate search for help.

Near shock, Willie stared transfixed at the lifeless form on the floor. Then, with the slow-witted comprehension of an animal that had just walked into a trap, he emitted a scream of rage and despair and ran back down the bloody staircase.

Pearl!

He must get back to Pearl. He must tell her what had happened, tell her the God-awful thing he had done. She'd know what to do. She'd help him. She was the only one left now to help him.

The truck was still running. He jumped in, shifted gears, and roared away down the hill toward the shack.

Pearl would know what to do.

13

Tom Penney fought to stay awake. As it always did lately, his rueful reflection on Willie had drained him physically and emotionally. Still, he admonished himself, *I must not sleep*. For with sleep came the dream. If he could just remain awake for these last few hours he would never have to suffer that horror again.

He tried to concentrate on other things, but like a torturer who delighted in tormenting his victim to the end, his brain would center only on the nightmare. He decided to let it come, to confront the demon face-to-face—but awake. Perhaps awake he could endure it. . . .

It had started two nights after *that* night. He was on the lam from Lexington and awakened in a cheap motel in Tallahassee in a cold sweat, his throat aching with the spasm of a suppressed scream. He sat on the edge of the bed and chain-smoked until the first light of a new day filtered through the window. Never before had he been able to recall a dream, but he remembered this one in detail, as if it were a horror movie and he was the unwilling star.

In the dream he was lying on his back on the floor in a strange place, his eyes fixed on a glowing globe-light fixture overhead. On all sides, wallpaper decorated with blooming daffodils extended from ceiling to floor to the gray rug on which he lay. As he stared, unable to divert his eyes, the light fixture transfigured into the head of a woman. Suddenly, the head exploded. Blood and brains splattered the room, obliterated the daffodils, and drenched his prostate body. He struggled to rise, but couldn't. Blood engulfed him. He coughed and gagged. He was drowning! He began to scream . . . and scream . . . and scream.

Then he awakened.

It happened again the following night. And the next. He began to drink. It didn't help.

He left Florida and fled west across Alabama, then Mississippi, trying to grab a few hours rest each night in some sleazy roadside inn. Some nights he'd park along a remote country lane, always far off the main highway, and sleep in the car. The dream followed, an unwelcome companion, always lurking just below the level of consciousness. He had read Freud and Jung. He needed no shrink to explain the dream's origins, or that it would eventually destroy him—unless he cheated the demon by destroying himself first. He had the means. He was armed. It was his only comforting thought.

Then, in Vicksburg, he met Pam.

He had stopped for gas. He avoided the larger stations with heavy traffic, seeking instead the small, out-of-the-way back-street garages. This one had an ancient pump with a glass well marked off in gallons on top that the attendant filled by pumping a handle at the base. When the well was full, the gas drained through the hose into the car. It was going to take a little time.

"Fill 'er up and check the oil." Tom looked around the place. "You got a crapper?"

The attendant removed the Buick's gas cap. "Outhouse, 'round back."

It was a stinking two-holer surrounded by piles of discarded tires, wrecked cars, and rusting engine parts. Tom pulled on the door and found it locked.

"Damn!" he complained, aloud.

"Keep your pants on, Buddy," someone inside yelled back. It was a female voice.

After a moment the door opened and a girl dressed in men's clothing stepped out. She was carrying a battered suitcase. She bowed at the waist and made a sweeping gesture toward the privy. "Be my guest."

When he came back around front the girl was standing near the car talking to the attendant. She smiled sweetly at Tom. "Feel better?"

"Sure. Seat was nice and warm."

"You're welcome. You heading west?"

"Yeah."

The attendant slammed the car hood down. "Oil and water're okay."

Tom paid the man. The girl said, "I could use a lift. I can't afford to pay, but I can drive."

Tom studied her for a moment. She was wearing a pair of twill pants and a blue, long-sleeve shirt. But other than attire there was nothing masculine about her. She was twenty, he guessed, not much more. Her auburn hair was cut in a bob, her hazel eyes sparkled when she talked, and she had one of those infectious smiles that toothpaste manufacturers loved to plaster on billboards. She was very pretty.

"Why not," he said. "Hop in."

She tossed the battered suitcase into the back seat. "My name's Pam. Pamelia, really. But who want's to be called that? You going as far as California?"

"Maybe."

"Say, great."

She jumped into the front seat and ran her hand across the dash. "You must be doing okay. You a salesman?"

Tom pulled away from the station. "Something like that. I travel, do all right for myself. How about you? You always picking up strangers? That could be dangerous, you know. No telling who's on the highways these days."

"No, this is the first time. Honest. I'm a pretty good judge of guys, though. I sized you up as an okay gent right off."

He stayed on Route 80 through Louisiana and drove the remainder of that afternoon without stopping. Pam entertained him with anecdotes about her life: a Southern upbringing in an overlarge family struggling to cope with the Depression, dropping out of school to work the day shift in the cotton mill in Jackson to help put food on the table.

"Why'd you leave?"

"Why, suh"—her voice drawled in a rich parody of a Southern Belle—"to save my honor."

Tom smiled.

She gave a lyrical laugh. "It's true. Old man Peterson—he's shop steward at the mill—he was always trying to get into my pants. He's got an office back of the looms, and the only girls who get ahead are the ones who'll play grab-ass with him on a beat-up old divan he keeps back there. I wouldn't play. He finally fired me."

"So you decided to run away?"

"Oh, I'm not running away. Sonny—he's my boy-friend—he's stationed in San Diego. He's a swabby. I'm going to join him there. Anyway, one less mouth to feed will be a blessing to Ma and Pa."

"You getting married?"

"Maybe. Maybe not. I get out there to California I just might decide to become one of those high-and-mighty movie stars." She laughed again.

Her cheerful spirit and good humor washed over Tom like a refreshing rain, cooling his parched soul. For the first time in days he felt at ease—and he found that he was laughing with her.

At nightfall they stopped at a drive-in cafe outside

Shreveport and Tom bought a sack of hamburgers and a couple of bottles of Coke. Two blocks further, he spotted a motel that looked cheap enough.

"Look, Pam, all I can afford is one room."

"Hey, that's okay."

He registered them under fake names as man and wife, although from the appearance of the place it was obvious that no one cared. He handed the clerk a twenty. The man frowned and went to the back room to make change.

There was a newspaper folded on the counter. While waiting for his money, Tom scanned the top section, then turned it over—and froze. A header above a story at the bottom of the front page read: MYSTERY CAR SOUGHT IN MILEY MURDERS.

Tom grabbed the paper and read:

Lexington, Ky. — Police officials here suspect that a 1941 blue Buick sedan used by two intruders fleeing the Lexington Country Club September 28 after murdering golf star Marion Miley and her mother, Elsie Miley, may have been stolen for use in the crime

Police report that an alert newsboy spotted the car when he delivered a paper at the club that morning. He described the car in detail.

The predominant theory is that two men broke into the club bent on robbery. They shot Mrs. Miley three times in the abdomen and Marion Miley twice, once in the back and once in the head.

Police have issued an all-points bulletin with a complete description of the car.

Tom's first thought was to flee, to drive toward the Gulf and ditch the Buick in the first remote swamp he came to. Then he remembered Pam.

"Damn!"

If he left without explanation it would raise suspicions, but if he checked out now and took her with him, he'd be hard pressed to explain why he was fleeing. She'd already seen the car.

What if she were to see the paper? Best to stay put for the night. He'd decide what to do with Pam tomorrow.

The room was what he'd expected: a dilapidated bed with a thin, lumpy mattress; shoddy chair; wash basin stained brown from a constantly dripping faucet.

Pam grabbed a Coke, then sat on the bed and dug into the sack for a burger. She handed one to Tom. He shook his head. "I'm not hungry."

She ate one sandwich and started on another. Tom dropped into the chair and sat there with a far-away look in his eyes.

"Why so glum all of a sudden?" Pam asked.

"Just tired, that's all."

She finished eating and switched off the light, leaving the room illuminated by moonlight that shined through a frayed curtain. She went to the bathroom. When she came out she was nude.

Despite the turmoil in his mind, Tom stared in awe. The ill-fitting clothing had been deceptive. Perhaps once in a lifetime, if the gods favored him, a man might meet a woman with a figure like this.

She came to him and held out her hand. "Come."

He undressed and crawled into the bed beside her. She turned and pressed her body toward him to ward off whatever demons were tormenting him.

Five minutes later he sat up on the side of the bed, his head in his hands.

Pam raised on an elbow and put a hand on his shoulder. "Hey . . . it's all right. That happens sometimes."

He stood. "Not to me, it doesn't."

He rummaged through his suitcase and took out a quart of Old Crow. He poured a tumbler half-full of bourbon and downed it as a thirst-crazed man might gulp water. Bottle in hand, he went to the chair and sat down. "Get some sleep. I'm going to sit up for a while."

Near midnight he sat bolt upright, soaked in sweat, awakened by a guttural noise from his own throat. Someone was shaking him. "Tom! Wake up! You're having a bad dream."

He looked up to see a woman's head hovering above him. Throwing an arm across his eyes he emitted a scream—a soul-piercing, primordial cry of the damned.

"Tom! It's me, Pam!"

He lowered his arm and stared at her blankly. Slowly, the blood-red fog cleared. He dropped his chin to his chest and began to sob.

She handed him the bottle and he drank from it again and again.

He awakened at mid-morning to find himself covered with the only blanket that had been on the bed. Pam was gone. Instinctively, he grabbed his pants from the floor and checked his wallet. He'd had two hundred dollars left after checking into the motel. It was all there.

His belly was afire. He went to the bathroom and gulped down glass after glass of foul-smelling water. Then he dressed, threw his stuff in the car, and drove off without stopping to eat. His head was pounding and waves of nausea racked his stomach. Each hangover was worse than the last. He drove slowly, scrutinizing each hitchhiker he passed. He never saw Pam again, but from that day on he would remember her as the refreshing spirit who brought a few shining hours of respite to the storm that was raging within him.

By the time he reached Dallas, ten days from the night he fled Lexington, his weight was down twenty pounds. His eyes seared like hot coals in sunken, galled sockets. His hands shook like those of a man afflicted with palsy. He could not continue to live with such torment.

That night in his motel he took the gun from his suitcase and shoved the barrel into his mouth. He sat that way for interminable minutes, frozen in time. He lowered the gun and uncapped his final bottle of bourbon. He drank long and hard, then raised the gun again. A half-dozen times that night he repeated the gesture—but he couldn't pull the trigger.

Next morning he sped through a stop sign in Fort Worth.

His first reaction on hearing the wailing siren and spotting the pursuing patrol car was relief. The running was over. When he pulled to the curb, one of the officers approached and asked for his drivers license. He handed it over without comment. The officer took the license to the patrol car to confer with his partner.

A dark thought crossed Penney's mind. Perhaps he could goad the police into doing what he could not. He watched intently through the rear-view mirror. Both officers were approaching. He reached beneath the seat, grabbed the pistol, and cocked it. It would be over in seconds. When he aimed at the cops, surely they would do the rest. Then, through the mirror, he saw one of the officers unsnap his holster and draw his gun. Tom's spine turned to jelly. He dropped the pistol, got out and thrust his hands into the air. "Yeah," he said, without waiting for the question, "I'm the one you're looking for."

While one of the officers frisked him, another thought took root in Tom's mind: *I'll just let the state of Kentucky kill me.*

The sound of the death house buzzer interrupted Tom's reverie. When Captain Rankin opened the gate, Tom heard the unmistakable voice of Warden Buchanan. "Get the key to Tom's cell and wait for me there. I'm going to talk to Bob first."

Puzzled, Tom stepped to the front of his cell.

At the other end of the corridor, Bob Anderson watched anxiously as the warden approached his cell. The big man's countenance was serious.

"Governor Johnson just called me, Bob," the warden said. "He's taking the position that any stay in your case must be a judicial decision, not an executive one."

Bob frowned. "I don't understand."

"It means that unless the courts are willing to reconsider your plea for a new trial, the governor won't intervene. In view of Tom's refusal to testify further, I'm afraid neither the state nor the federal courts will reconsider."

Bob's face drained of color. Trembling with frustration and rage, he sat down on his bed. "So, the fix is in. There's nothing Johnson will do, nothing the courts will do. How about that,

Warden? The whole crazy system is geared to let an innocent man die."

There was no adequate response. The warden said, "I'll be back one more time before tonight. If you want to talk to me before then, tell Captain Rankin."

He didn't relay the governor's personal comment on the case: "There's only one person who can save Bob Anderson now, Jess—and that's Tom Penney."

The warden paused briefly at the middle cell. "How are you, Willie?"

"Okay, I reckon. Tom's preacher's coming to see me tonight. We're gonna pray." Willie revealed the news proudly.

"Good. I'm glad. I'll be back to see you later this afternoon."

Tom was standing at the bars when the warden approached his cell. "Tom, I'm coming in to talk to you."

Tom stepped aside while Captain Rankin opened the cell door then locked the warden inside. The warden turned the wooden chair around and sat down. Tom sat on the bed facing him. The warden noticed the pile of letters on the bed. "Looks like you've been busy."

"Yes sir." Tom knew the warden hadn't come to talk about his correspondence.

"I understand Father Libs is coming to be with you tonight. Willie says he's looking forward to seeing him, too."

Tom nodded. "Father Donnelly couldn't get leave. I'm sorry about that, but it doesn't make any real difference. Father Libs will prepare the Eucharist."

He reached into his desk drawer and took out a folded napkin. He opened it gently and showed the warden the thin wafer of bread he had kept there for days. "Sister Magdalene sent it to me—from Saint Gertrude's Monastery in Detroit. It will be my final host."

The warden nodded. "Many people are praying for you today, Tom."

Tom refolded the napkin around the wafer and put it back in the drawer. "Yes. The Church has arranged for me to be buried in holy ground in Lexington—Hill Crest. I have been richly blessed."

"So Father Donnelly tells me. He says you've come further in a year than most do in a lifetime. He says you're a sincere convert."

"And he's right," Tom said emphatically.

"Good. Because that's what I came to talk to you about. As you know, I've been considering the order of execution tonight—"

"Warden," Tom interceded, "if that's what's on your mind, don't let it bother you. I know that the law says Bob should go first. I also know you decided some days ago that I should go first. I've accepted that. I'm prepared for it."

"Yes. Well, I *had* considered that. But on second thought, I've decided against it. We're going to do what the law says. We'll follow the order of conviction—Bob first, then you, then Willie."

There was a flicker of misgiving in Tom's eyes. "I . . . I'm afraid I don't understand."

The warden leaned forward and fixed Tom with a no-nonsense stair. His voice became steel. "Tom, it came to me that if Bob is innocent, you may have convinced yourself that if you die first, while he's still alive, then his death won't be on your conscience. You couldn't do anything to stop it, could you? It would be beyond your control You could have reasoned that in that case, your salvation wouldn't be threatened."

Tom started to speak.

The warden silenced him with a raised hand. "But, if Bob dies first, while you're still alive, that would make things different, wouldn't it? If you *have* railroaded him, and you stand mute while he dies, then there'll be no question who's responsible, will there? In that case, his death will be on your conscience—*and on your soul.*"

The warden sat back in the chair. "The Mileys died before you converted. Their deaths were no test of your faith. But Bob's death *is* going to be a test of it. I'm going to make certain of that. He goes first tonight."

After a long silence, the warden asked, "Is there anything

you want to say to me about that right now?"

The long scar across Tom's face drained chalk-white and the muscles in his jaw began to twitch. He diverted his eyes from the warden's piercing stare. "I have . . . taken a holy vow . . . to say nothing more about the case."

The warden stood. "Very well. I guess that's the way it's going to be. Tom, you testified at Bob's trial that he was guilty. Then you got religion and announced to the world that you had lied about Bob and that Buford Stewart was your accomplice. Next, you came to me in confidence and said that you lied about Stewart. Then you clammed up and refused to testify in court or talk anymore about the case to anyone. All right. I don't know if Bob is guilty or not. But you sure as hell do. And if you have *borne false witness* against him, I want you to think about this, and think hard for the few hours you have left: From the moment Bob steps out of his cell tonight you'll have about ninety seconds to save his life—and save your soul from eternal damnation. It's in your hands now."

The warden called for Captain Rankin to open the cell and left.

Tom Penny reached beneath his pillow and withdrew his rosary. Gripping it tightly, he curled into a fetal ball on his bed and wept.

14

Pearl Smith lay across the bed in the second-floor room in Knoth's Hotel, shivering beneath a thin blanket. Chilled by a sudden sprinkle during her walk from the River View Inn, she had removed her outer clothing and hung it over the heat vent in the floor to dry, then wrapped herself in the blanket to try to nap. The frigid rain, following the overlong bus ride from Louisville, had left her drained. But sleep wouldn't come. After a while she moved a chair close to the heat vent, pulled the blanket tightly around her, and sat looking out the window. Up and down the narrow street below, people were entering and leaving shops, buying their weekly ration of gas at the Standard Oil station on the corner, or merely going about their daily routines as if there were nothing more momentous impending in their quaint little town this evening than the Eddyville-vs.-Fredonia softball game the hand-printed placards in store windows announced was scheduled to begin play in the town park at 8:00 P.M.

* Pearl wondered if she was hungry. Except for the cup of coffee at the little cafe when she got off the bus earlier that afternoon, she had eaten nothing except a small sweet roll before leaving Louisville at dawn. She'd always been indifferent to food and could go for days on one meal a day, usually no more than a sandwich or a bowl of soup. Even so, she knew she should eat something. She thought about walking back up the hill to the cafe for a snack, but discarded the idea. It was too near the prison. She would see that abominable institution again soon enough. Maybe later she go across the street to the grocery store and get an apple or a banana. That would be all she'd need. But for the time being, she decided to remain here in her rented room, trying to keep warm.

She thought back on her life with the man who had caused her to make this trip, the sad little man with the defeated countenance who had remained after her show two summers ago to compliment her act. Willie Baxter was one of the ugliest men she'd ever seen. Yet there was a fragility, some unspoken need in him that kindled an instinct in her she had never known before. It wasn't maternal. God knows, nothing maternal held any appeal for her. Perhaps it was no more than the attraction of one loser to another.

"Pearl, how'd you lose your ear?" Willie had asked her one night soon after they met.

She'd promised to tell him someday. She never had, and he'd never asked again. She wondered how he would have reacted to the story—the whole lousy, rotten story. . . .

On her fourteenth birthday Pearl Smith's virginity was sold at auction at her mother's whorehouse in Cincinnati. The high bidder was an army master sergeant from Fort Thomas, just across the Ohio River in Kentucky. The sergeant had suggested the auction after months of ogling the small dark-haired girl who changed the linens in the upstairs bedrooms after every fourth or fifth tryst. Pearl's mother insisted on postponing the sale until her daughter turned fourteen. Pearl's mother had scruples.

By the time she was sixteen, Pearl was the most sought-after girl in the house. More sensual than pretty, she was versatile at her work, and young. It was an unbeatable combination, but a fleeting one, and Mama Smith set out to make the best of a good thing while it lasted. She raised Pearl's price to $10 for a quarter-hour and allowed her to keep twenty-five percent of her earnings. On a good night Pearl could make $50 for herself and $150 for the house. In a show of maternal good will, Mama charged Pearl fifty cents a day less for room and board than she charged the other girls.

Pearl perfected her skills at Mama's for six years. Then, shortly after her twentieth birthday, Mama sold her across the river to the notorious Elwood "Doc" Watson.

In certain circles of Bluegrass society, Doc Watson was hailed as a man of vision. An affable, dapper little man who affected a snow-white goatee, spats, and a gold-handled walking cane, he recruited the most beautiful girls he could find. Then, in a daring show of entrepreneurship, he confined operations to a single month out of the year—two weeks before and the two weeks following the Kentucky Derby.

No other event in the country could match the Kentucky Derby for attracting a multitude of high rollers to one city at one time. For days preceding the annual "Run for the Roses," Louisville became one grand carnival. Merry-makers descended on every bar in town vying for the privilege of buying round after round, often paying with hundred-dollar bills peeled from a fist-cramping wad indiscreetly carried in a trouser pocket. It was a con artist's dream, a pickpocket's mother load, a pimp's paradise.

In the hierarchy of Derby week hookers, Doc Watson's girls were in a class of their own. The merely well-to-do couldn't afford them. But the rich, the powerful, and the corporations that curried favor with them were willing to pay high premium for discretion. Doc's girls contracted out for $100 an hour, twenty-four-hour minimum, $1,000 retainer in advance. Most were consigned months ahead for the entire four weeks. With a dozen girls under contract, Doc's annual gross for his unique operation averaged $800,000. He paid his girls $30,000 each for a month's work and allowed them to keep all gratuities. He put half his profits into blue-chip stocks and used the rest to travel the brothel circuit, recruiting fresh talent.

Pearl's reputation had spread through the grapevine to Louisville. Though her looks weren't up to Doc's usual standards, he wasn't one to dismiss an outstanding talent. He paid Mama Smith $5,000 for her daughter, brought Pearl down from Cincinnati, and treated her to a complete image and wardrobe make-over. She was an instant hit.

During the five years she worked for Doc, Pearl became accustomed to high living. Her income each spring, plus generous tips from clients, provided her with a fashionable apartment near Cherokee Park and freedom to enjoy life in style for the remainder of the year. Her future looked secure.

Then, she got greedy.

It didn't take a lot of smarts for Pearl to figure that at $100 an hour she was putting close to $70,000 a year into Doc's coffers. And he was paying her less than half that. She decided to eliminate the middle man.

The following January she informed Doc that she wouldn't be working that year. "Perhaps next year," she murmured. Next day she sent word to a couple of Doc's affluent clients that she'd be freelancing the Derby that May.

The first weekend before the Derby, she was working the Post and Paddock lounge near Churchill Downs when two prosperously dressed men approached and propositioned her for an all-night ménage à trois.

"It'll cost you double," she said.

The men agreed. "We're at the Brown Hotel," one of them said. "I'll bring the car around."

She was stepping into the car when a sharp blow on the back of her neck rendered her unconscious. Sometime later, she awoke on the rear floor of a moving vehicle with her mouth taped shut and her hands tied behind her back. Her neck ached from the rabbit punch that had put her out. Someone's foot was pressed against her head, holding her down.

After what seemed an eternity, the car stopped. The larger of the two men who had abducted her removed his foot from her head, opened the back door, and got out. "Okay, girlie, this is your stop."

He pulled her from the car. Then he and his companion dragged her across a large gravel bed to the pit of an abandoned rock quarry. The big man locked his arms around her from behind. "Let's get this over with," he said. "It's spooky out here."

She heard the click of a switchblade, then spotted the open knife in the smaller man's hand. Her struggles against the bearhug were futile. The smaller man pushed her head down, then grasped the top of her right ear and pulled outward. With two quick slices he severed the ear from her head. The large man pushed her away, hard.

She fell on her back in the gravel. The pain was unbearable. She tried to scream, but the gag muffled her cries.

The little man cleaned his knife on Pearl's dress, then wrapped her ear in a paper bag and put it in his pocket. He reached down and grabbed her by the hair and yanked her face upward. "Awright, sister, I got a message for you from Doc, so listen up. He says to tell you that you try freelancing around here again, or anywhere else, and next time it'll be your throat. Got that?"

Pearl sobbed.

The man yanked her hair again, hard. "I asked you a question, dammit!"

Pearl nodded.

The two men left.

She lay there in pain, sobbing, humiliated, ravished. At last she made it to her feet and stumbled back across the gravel bed to the ditch below the highway, where she fainted.

She awoke at dawn, looking up into the face of a startled highway worker. He had removed her bonds. "I'm gonna call the cops."

"No!" Pearl begged. "Please."

He dressed her wounds from a first-aid kit he carried in his truck, then drove her to a suburban bus station where she caught a taxi. She went to her bank and withdrew her savings. At her apartment she threw what she could carry into one bag, then took a bus to Cincinnati.

Mama Smith was appalled. "You can stay the night, then you gotta git. I don't want no trouble with the likes of Doc Watson."

For the next six years Pearl worked the small towns around Fort Knox—Radcliff, Shepherdsville, Elizabethtown, Vine Grove—turning just enough back-alley tricks on military payday to keep her in room and board. She stayed constantly on the move, sticking to small, cheap hotels away from the main stream, never checking into the same one twice. Wherever she went, she was always glancing over her shoulder for the man with the switchblade.

One day in Bardstown she spotted a sign tacked to a telephone pole:

HELP WANTED, FEMALE — EXOTIC DANCER
EXPERIENCE UNNECESSARY. APPLY IN PERSON.

The sign gave a phone number in Louisville.

She applied and got the job.

Within a year she had conceived and perfected her act as Lola LaRue in "Rape of the Maiden." For the first time since that terrible night in the rock quarry, she breathed easy. She was attracting enough rubes off the midway to keep her head above water, she wasn't risking a throat slashing by turning tricks, and she didn't have to sleep with anyone at the carnival as part of the deal.

Such was her life that summer night in Lexington when a melancholy little man with a defeated countenance remained one night after one of her shows to compliment her.

After their first few dates, during which Willie made no passes at her, she decided to take him to bed. The decision surprised her as much as it did him. She had never given sex freely, had never regarded it as anything more than a business commodity. Since that night in Cincinnati years before, when her mother had auctioned her off to that foul-smelling sergeant from Fort Thomas, she had sold her body to thousands of men. Yet Willie, the ferret-faced junkie with the sad eyes, was the only man she had ever "made love" to. It was new, it was different, it was exciting. For the first time she knew what it was to share her body with a man for warmth and affection rather than cold cash.

From the beginning, she recognized the depth of feeling Willie had for her. As summer passed she began to harbor hopes for the future that only weeks before would have been absurd. Perhaps she could start anew with Willie. Perhaps together they could find the pleasures of life that separately they had missed. It was a precious thought, new and heady, and she realized with an insight that made her glow that for the first time in her life she was truly happy.

Then came the night she was awakened by the sound of gunfire—and their world turned sour again.

She had paced the floor that night after Willie went to investigate, anxiously wondering what was taking him so long. At last she heard the truck come racing back down the hill an hour or more after he left. Then the door flew open and he rushed inside. He stood in the middle of the floor, his face ashen, his mouth moving without making words. His eyes mirrored unspeakable horror.

Pearl threw off the covers and ran to him and put her arms around him. He was racked with tremors.

"Willie! What's wrong?"

"He . . . he . . . shot her. . . . " His voice was a guttural whisper.

"He? Who? Shot who?"

"Mrs. Miley . . . she's . . . dead." He finally looked at her. "Jesus, Pearl . . . she's dead!"

She led him to a chair and made him sit. He wasn't a hard-liquor man, but she poured a shot of bourbon from a bottle she kept on hand and made him drink it down. He coughed and rubbed his lips and she made him drink another. Then she knelt on the floor and took his hands in hers. "Now, tell me what happened. . . . What did you see?"

Slowly, the story came out. He told her about telling Tom about the money one day last summer, how Tom had begged him to help steal it, how Tom convinced him to leave the clubhouse door unlocked, how he'd forgotten to do that, how Tom had promised to split the loot so that Willie could show Pearl a good time. Finally, he told her about the ghastly thing he'd found upstairs in the clubhouse apartment.

"Oh, Pearl," he wailed, "I done a God-awful thing. I killed her!" He clutched her arms. "Pearl . . . what am I gonna do?"

The door was still open. She loosened his grip, walked over to the door, and kicked it shut with her bare foot. Then she raised a clinched fist above her head and swore at the top of her voice, "THAT STINKING . . . ROTTEN . . . SON OF A BITCH!"

She stood there shaking with rage until the emotion drained from her. Then she went back to Willie and stood in front of him so that he would have to look up at her, as a child would to an adult.

"You're not going to do a damned thing," she said firmly. "*You* didn't kill her. Tom killed her. It's his rap. We're going to stay here, together. You understand?"

"But . . . but the cops, Pearl. They're gonna question me for sure. What about the cops?"

"When the cops come . . . we'll cross that bridge."

He nodded obediently.

And so they stayed together. She did her shows and returned to the shack as soon as the last act was over. He did his chores around the greens, answered police inquiries about his whereabouts that night, and Pearl backed him up. She didn't lie. He *was* in the shack with her. Willie didn't mention Tom, nor did the police. He learned with surprise that the body he'd found that night was not Mrs. Miley, but her daughter, Marion. That fact made the murders international news. He and Pearl clung to each other, made love, hoped. She promised to stick by him, whatever came, to the end.

The news of Tom's arrest in Texas sent shivers through them. Then, when Tom fingered Bob Anderson without mentioning Willie, their hopes soared. *Perhaps,* Pearl thought, *I misjudged Tom.* Maybe she and Willie *would* have the new life they dreamed of.

Two days later in Lexington, Tom told police that Raymond Baxter, too, was an accomplice.

And the dream was over.

Now, in her room at Knoth's Hotel, Pearl thought ahead to what she must do that evening. She remembered the map in her coat pocket. She got up and retrieved it and was pleased to find it hadn't gotten wet. Gary, who ran the carrousel at the carnival, had drawn it for her. Gary was familiar with Eddyville. He'd served four years up on the hill in Jesse Buchanan's College of Hard Knocks. She studied the simple hand drawing again, as she had a dozen times on the bus. It was simple. There was no way to make a mistake. She put the map back in her coat pocket and sat back to wait for the hours to pass.

She hoped it wouldn't be raining that night.

15

Allan Trout, chief correspondent for *The Courier-Journal,* Frankfort Bureau, was a highly esteemed reporter on the staff of one of the most venerable newspapers in America. He arrived at Eddyville in mid-afternoon. With an unlimited C-ration book for gasoline, he decided to make the eight-hour drive from Frankfort rather than take the train or bus, as most of his colleagues had done. He came alone. He preferred to drive alone, liked the solitude if offered him to think, to mentally compose his work for the weeks to come. And he needed time to think today. Late in his career he had taken an interest in criminology, particularly the pros and cons of capital punishment. He had researched all capital cases in Kentucky, and many in other states, and had followed developments in the Miley case from the day of the murders. He had a personal interest in it. He had been a fan of

Marion Miley and, along with a multitude of other fans, had followed her around the course during what turned out to be her final two major tournaments. Later, he had gotten to know her personally.

Trout, a slender, well-tailored man who approached his reportorial chores with a genteel dignity, thought back to that day eighteen months earlier when he had driven from Frankfort to Lexington to interview Kentucky's most outstanding woman golfer—the Kentuckian who, for the past nine years, had ranked with the foremost American women in the game. It had been a difficult interview to arrange. A popular favorite on the tournament circuit, Marion Miley was away from home more often than not. He finally caught her in residence at the country club on the last weekend in August.

It was a typical midwest summer day, and Marion's mother, Elsie, made a pitcher of lemonade for her daughter and guest to sip to ward off the sweltering heat. She'd also baked cookies earlier in the cool of the morning, from a recipe she had developed using Kentucky-grown and rendered sorghum molasses. She insisted that Trout have one. He found it delicious, and she gave him a sack of them to take home.

Trout and Marion took the lemonade and a couple of glasses to an umbrella-covered table beside the putting green. They chatted aimlessly for a while, establishing a rapport before getting down to the purpose of the visit. He had called her Miss Miley and she'd insisted he call her Marion. During the course of that preamble he learned that her passion for golf was matched only by her love of horses.

"Of course," she said, "for a Kentucky girl, especially one living in Bluegrass country, that's almost obligatory, don't you think?"

He began to quote: "Show me a land where men have no use for horses . . . "

She picked it up: " . . . and I'll show you a land where there are no men."

They both laughed.

"You realize, don't you," Marion remarked with pride,

"that you're not the only journalist here today?"

It was a reference to an assignment she had recently fulfilled as special correspondent for *The Lexington Leader*, covering the Women's National Golf Tournament at Brookline, Massachusetts.

"That's right," Trout recalled. "I read your report. Very well done, indeed."

She thanked him for the compliment.

He had enjoyed the preliminary banter and found the lithe, handsome young woman with close-cut black hair and a quick smile to be personable and easy to talk to. Finally, he brought out his pad and got to the question he'd come for. "Tell me, Miss Miley . . ."

"Marion," she chided, and shook a finger at him.

"Oh, yes . . . Marion. Tell me, speaking of golf now, how would you define your goals?"

She took a sip of lemonade, then flashed a captivating smile. "To become the best woman golfer in the world." The smile turned impish. "Then to challenge the men."

He couldn't have asked for a better quote. They shared another laugh, and he agreed that it was indeed an excellent plan.

Four weeks later, her dreams came to a horrifying end.

Who could have believed, Trout thought as he drove toward Eddyville, that the lovely, high-spirited young athlete he interviewed that sunny day would soon be a victim in a gruesome double murder.

And tonight would be the culmination of the case—the execution of the killers. He wanted to talk to Warden Buchanan about that before the press of commitments this evening commanded all the warden's time.

He turned his thoughts to the warden. He had known Buchanan since the big man first came to Frankfort to join the staff of Governor Ruby LaFoon. Later, soon after Buchanan gave up the U.S. Marshal's job to take over the prison at Eddyville, an incident occurred that compelled Trout to seek an interview with the new warden.

Seven months after Warden Buchanan began his tenure at

Eddyville, a judge in Greenup County sentenced a fifteen-year-old boy convicted of car theft to three years in the maximum security prison at Eddyville. The boy arrived at the institution shackled between two deputy sheriffs, and scared to death. Buchanan refused to accept him.

Dumbfounded, the two deputies had no alternative but to return the boy to Greenup County, where the enraged judge declared that "the warden's head will roll!"

Next morning, Governor Chandler called Warden Buchanan for an explanation. The warden stated his belief that the boy's offense, his first and only one, did not warrant him being incarcerated with hardened criminals. "The day the courts start sending kids like him to this institution," he declared, "is the day I leave."

The following week the boy was resentenced to the minimum-security reformatory near Louisville.

Discussing the incident with Trout, Buchanan said, "Allan, I'm convinced that there are first offenders who could be rehabilitated without them ever spending a day in prison. Turn them over to me for one hour. Let me take them on a tour of this institution, show them what they'd be facing, who they'd be living with inside these walls. Then I'd kick their butts down the front steps with a warning never to come back. I don't believe you'd see them inside a courtroom again."

Though neither Buchanan nor Trout were acquainted with the term at that time, the warden was describing what in later years penal psychologists would proclaim as the "newly developed" theory of "shock probation."

Based on that interview and others that followed, Trout summed up Warden Buchanan's attributes as considerate, astute, helpful, concerned, authoritative, sometimes intimidating, but above all, fair. They were all adjectives he would use at one time or another to describe the man. In time, he came to consider himself and Jess Buchanan good friends, and he knew that the warden felt the same.

The gate guard signed Trout in, then said, "The warden would like to see you before you go to the reporters room, Mister

Trout."

Henry Sproule ushered Trout directly into the warden's office. The warden stood and shook hands. As always, Trout was awed at the sight of his gargantuan friend rising from his chair. As he once wrote, "The warden stood up . . . and up . . . and up."

"Good to see you again, Allan," the warden said. "Glad you came early. I'd like to talk to you for a minute." He indicated a chair and Trout sat.

The warden indicated some papers on his desk. "I've been reading over 'To Kill or Not to Kill.' Looks like you've been doing your homework."

Trout had been planning to do a feature article on capital punishment for months. He'd mailed a draft of the work he'd done so far to the warden a week before.

"There's still a lot more to be done," Trout said. "I was hoping for your comments."

Buchanan nodded. Then, without further commentary on the proposed column, he said, "Allan, there're going to be about forty reporters here tonight. Several are already in the reporters room. I'd like for you to ride herd on them for me; let them know the rules. Will you do that?"

"Anyway I can be of help," Trout agreed.

"Let them know they're free to come and go at will on this side of the back gate. No one is permitted beyond that point unless they're with me or a designated guard. The prison cook will serve supper in the reporters room around five. It's the same food served on the inmate line—stew tonight. Some of them might want to make that part of their story. If prison food doesn't suit them, they can get a meal outside. There're no Louisville-style restaurants around here, just a cafe across the road and a diner in town at the foot of the hill. There's also a hotel of sorts, for those who aren't catching the train tonight."

Trout nodded. He had heard most of what the warden was saying before, but let him speak without interruption.

"Those taking the night train will be in a bit of a rush. The executions are scheduled to begin just after midnight. It should all be over by one o'clock, most likely earlier. That'll give them a half-hour or so to make it to the Kuttawa depot. I'll have cars standing by to take them."

"I brought my own car," Trout said. "I can drive some of them to the depot."

The warden picked up his cigar humidor and offered a White Owl to Trout. Trout declined.

The warden lit up. "There's a fellow in the reporters room I'm concerned about. Pretty shaky, looks about twenty. I don't know who sent him . . . up from Nashville, I think. I've asked Deputy Warden Lady to sit beside him in the death house tonight, just in case. Meanwhile, I think it would be wise if you'd brief him on what he's in for down there. Explain that it's not like covering an automobile accident, for example. That's messy sometimes, but after-the-fact. Executions are . . . well, you're an eye witness to the snuffing out of a human life. It's not an easy thing to do . . . I mean, to *watch*," the warden quickly corrected himself. "And tonight there're going to be three of them. I'm not sure that young fellow's up to it. You understand what I'm trying to say?"

The warden's slip of the tongue didn't escape Trout, and he wondered about it. "I understand, Jess. I'll talk to him."

"I'll be going to the death house in a few minutes to read the death warrants for the last time. If any of the reporters want to, they can go along. As for interviewing the condemned men, that's up to the men. They can ask, but I don't want anyone trying to hassle those fellows."

The warden knocked the ash from his cigar. "That about does it, Allan. Any questions?"

"Jess, do you think Bob Anderson is guilty?"

Stony silence. He had caught the warden off guard and Buchanan's expression showed it.

His tone now coolly official, the warden replied, "Allan, I'm an instrument of the courts. It's not my place to question guilt or innocence."

It was an evasion, and Trout knew it. Everything the warden had said up to now, everything they had talked about in previous conversations, told him that Jess Buchanan could not be all that detached from the most intriguing question in the most infamous murder case in Kentucky history. Trout wondered if he should press for a more definitive answer. He decided to let it ride—for the moment.

He stood. "I'll go get the herd straightened out. I'll be here if you need to talk."

The "reporters room" was so called only on the day of a newsworthy occurrence at the prison. On other days it served as the warden's conference room or a meeting place for the parole board. Most executions weren't newsworthy. The majority of men who died in the electric chair at Eddyville—no woman had ever suffered that fate—shared their final moments with no one other than the warden, the death house supervisor, the prison chaplain, and the designated guards. But tonight the notorious Miley murderers were to pay their debt to society. *That* was news. There were a dozen reporters in the room when Allan Trout entered. That number would more than triple before nightfall.

The room was spacious. A long mahogany table with matching chairs sat in mid-floor. A side table against one wall bore a telephone, a coffee pot, tableware, and condiments. Four men were playing cards at the conference table. Others were talking or reading. Several greeted Trout.

At the far end of the room a young man sat with his back turned to his colleagues, staring out the window. As Trout watched, the man pulled a flask from his inside coat pocket, took a swig from it, and hastily replaced it. One of the other reporters who had seen the furtive drink looked up at Trout and shook his head.

Trout approached the young man. The charcoal smell of scotch intercepted him from six feet away. "Son," Trout said, "if Warden Buchanan finds out you've smuggled that flask in here he'll send you packing. You'll lose your accreditation here for sure."

The young man regarded Trout through blurred eyes. "Mister, I'm sure as hell not going down to that pig-sticking tonight cold sober."

Trout shook his head and went to join his colleagues at the table.

A few minutes later, Warden Buchanan entered the room. He was wearing his coat and hat. In his right hand was a heavy hickory walking cane with a steel tip. Trout nudged the man nearest him. "See that cane," he said, voice low. "He always carries it when he goes into the prison yard. And woe to any convict who approaches him closer than the length of it. It's the best-known unwritten rule in the institution."

For a moment, the warden looked curiously at the young man at the window, who was still staring outward, oblivious to all. The warden turned to the others. "I'm on my way to the death house to read the warrants of execution. Any of you who want may come along. First, you should know that I received a call from Governor Johnson earlier about Anderson's request for a stay. It's been denied."

Two reporters at the end of the table made a grab for the single telephone on the buffet. The warden stopped them. "There're enough phones for all. You can use my office, and the deputy's. You should know, too, that I've already informed Bob."

"How'd he take it, Warden?" one reporter asked.

"Hard."

"Do you believe this is the final word?" another asked.

"Yes," the warden replied.

"What about Penney, Warden? Did the governor say anything about Penney?"

"No."

Once again he refused to reveal the governor's comment that only Tom Penney could save Bob Anderson now.

As always when he passed through the huge barred gate leading from the security of the administration building into the prison yard, Allan Trout felt apprehensive. The first time he had done so, soon after Warden Buchanan took office, he had comforted himself beforehand with the thought that he would be surrounded by guards. Instead, he had been accompanied by one man—the warden. Now, as he had on that earlier occasion, he realized there was no other person he would rather be with at such times than this towering legend of a lawman.

As they walked through the eight-acre walled-in yard greening in the mild late-winter weather with well-tended grassy slopes and freshly pruned shrubs, Trout watched the hardest of Kentucky's hardcore criminal element step aside, hat in hand, to give the warden wide berth. He spoke to each man, calling him by name. Only then would the inmates return his greeting.

Trout, his feature on capital punishment much in mind, was the only reporter who asked to go along for the final reading of the death warrants. Entering Cellblock One, they passed through the three oldest cellblocks in the prison until they reached the eastern extension of Cellblock Three. There the warden pushed a buzzer beside a barred door much smaller than the other gates at the institution. This was the entryway to the death house. When Captain Rankin unlocked the door, the warden introduced Trout, whom Rankin recognized from previous visits.

Trout noted that the death house had been freshly painted, and knew the touch was the work of the warden's wife. When Warden Buchanan first came to Eddyville, the death house resembled a dismal dungeon more fitting to the era of Marquis de Sade than to twentieth-century America. Mrs. Buchanan undertook to change that. With her husband's blessing, she had the walls of the cells, hallway, and even the death chamber washed, sanitized, and painted. She had the bare floor of the hallway and death chamber tiled, then added curtains to the death cell windows. Although none of the improvements could belie the grim purpose of the annex, they were nonetheless appreciated by everyone.

Warden Buchanan stepped to the first cell. Trout followed and fixed his eyes on the beefy, dark-haired man standing there at the bars—Bob Anderson, the controversial question mark in the Marion Miley murder case.

The warden pulled a document from his coat pocket. "Bob, the law requires that prior to your execution, I must read the court warrant to you for a final time."

Anderson looked at the warden without comment.

The warden adjusted his glasses and read:

> Commonwealth of Kentucky, Plaintiff
> versus
> Robert H. Anderson, Defendant
>
> The defendant having been brought into court and informed of the nature of the indictment, plea and

verdict, and asked if he had any legal cause to show why judgement should not be pronounced against him; and none being shown, it is adjudged by the court that the defendant be remanded to the custody of the sheriff of Fayette County and that the sheriff shall safely convey and deliver him to the warden of the State Penitentiary at Eddyville, there to be safely kept until the twenty-sixth day of February, nineteen-hundred-and-forty-three, on which day and before sunrise, the warden or his deputy within the confines of said penitentiary shall cause to pass through his body a current of electricity of sufficient intensity to cause death as soon as possible, and the application of such current shall continue until death ensures.

The warden cleared his throat, folded the paper, and handed it to Captain Rankin. If Bob Anderson felt any emotion on hearing his death warrant read, his countenance did not reveal it.

The warden's face did. The readings were an odious duty that he loathed, just as he loathed writing the legally required notice-of-execution letters to the next of kin: "It is my sad but official duty to inform you that unless executive or judicial authorities intervene, your (son/husband/father) will be put to death by legal electrocution on Friday the . . . "

The warden said, "Bob, unless you ask, this is the last time I'll see you before tonight. God be with you."

With a terse grunt, Bob went to his bed, lay back, and turned his eyes to the ceiling.

Tom Penney was waiting at the front of his cell. When the warden finished reading the warrant in Tom's name, he asked, "Tom, is there anything you want to say to me now . . . in private, perhaps?"

The tall, scar-faced man with the rueful brown eyes was gripping the bars so tightly his knuckles were bloodless. "No sir," he replied.

The warden hesitated, as if he expected more. "If you change your mind, I'll be available. Otherwise, I won't see you again before tonight. God be with you."

"And with you, Warden," Tom replied softly.

The cryptic exchange puzzled Trout. Something beyond routine was going on here. He decided not to ask the warden for an explanation—yet.

At the middle cell the warden repeated the reading of the warrant to Willie. The little man smiled throughout, as if he were listening to a nanny recite a bedtime story. When the warden finished, Willie nodded. "Much obliged, Warden," he said with deep feeling.

"You're welcome, Willie. God be with you."

At the exit gate the warden said, "Captain Rankin, Allan is going to stay with you for a while. He'd like to interview you about a feature he's doing. He'd also like to talk to the condemned men. I've already told him that's up to them, but I have no objection if he wants to ask. Deputy Lady will be down later to escort him back up front. If you need me I'll be in my office, or Sproule will know where to find me."

The warden left the death house.

Captain Rankin led Trout to his office. "Coffee, Allan?"

"Sounds good. Black." Trout sat in a chair near the captain's desk.

Captain Rankin filled two cups from the pot he kept going, handed a cup to Trout, then sat down at his desk. "Warden says you're doing a feature?"

"On capital punishment. Jess has been helping me. He says you're the only person to ever hold the job of death house supervisor."

Captain Rankin nodded. "That's right."

"Then you've witnessed every execution here."

"Every one."

"Can you tell me something about those men? Statistics, details, personal insights perhaps. I thought you might have some records on file."

Captain Rankin swiveled back in his chair. "Don't need any records on file. You got a tablet?"

Trout pulled out a small notebook and pen.

"Statistics," Captain Rankin repeated. "Well, let's see. All told there've been a hundred and twenty-four—sixty-six Negroes, fifty-eight white. First was Jimmy Buckner, eighteen-year-old lad from Marion County."

Trout made a quick calculation. Fifty-three percent of the men executed in Kentucky were Negroes, in a state with less than a third Negro population. He made a note to do a follow-up study on the ramifications of that telling ratio.

"Personal insights?" Captain Rankin continued. "Well, they were an odd lot, they were. Let's see. Black Texas—now there's a story for you. Been a soldier. He went on a fourteen-day robbery and shooting spree between Dallas and Louisville. Killed eight men and three women. He had a teenage nephew doing time in the reformatory up in Frankfort. Smart-alecky kid, sour on the world, vowed to avenge his uncle as soon as he got out. Black Texas heard about the boy's bragging and asked to have him brought down here to witness the execution. Kid swaggered in here cocky as a banty rooster. Fifteen minutes later he stumbled out meek as a lamb. Instant rehabilitation, I tell you."

Trout made hasty notes.

"Whispering Dan. Had the most beautiful singing voice I ever heard on a man—Irish tenor, I guess you'd call it. Sang gospel songs day and night. Started singing while they were strapping him into the chair. Was singing 'Rock of Ages' when the shock hit him. 'Let me hide myself in Thee . . . '—those were his last words.

"Pegleg Pete. Pete loved to dance. Could tap out a tune on that wooden leg better than most tappers do with two feet. They took away his peg when they strapped him in. Last thing he said was, 'Looks like this gonna be old Pete's last dance.' When the shock hit him that stump began to jump up and down, just like it was keeping time with the dynamo.

"Showboat. Now there was a puzzling case. Found him drunk one day, right down there in that end cell that Tom Penney's in now. We searched every nook and cranny of it, couldn't find a thing. All his mail and packages were censored. No one could get close enough to that high window in his cell to slip him anything. He just smiled at our questions, said he had no intention of dying sober. All we could do was scratch our heads. Few weeks later, there he was again, higher than a Chinese kite. Same search. Same result. Well, I started keeping a closer eye on him. I'd sneak into the dynamo room across the hall where I could see into his cell but he couldn't see me. He always saved a bit of bread from his meal to feed the pigeons that came to roost on his cell window. Nothing wrong with that. Now, those pigeons used to feed all day down at the prison farm before coming back here to roost. Well, sir, one night I saw Showboat grab one of those birds and start squeezing it's craw. Sure enough, that bird coughed up a few grains of corn. And that's how he was doing it. When he'd collected enough corn, he'd add some of the sugar I'd let him have for his morning coffee, mash it all up and mix it with water. After a while it got just ripe enough to give him a buzz. We put a screen over his window and that ended that. He died sober, by the way."

Captain Rankin got up and refilled his cup. He held the pot toward Trout, who declined. The captain returned to his chair. "The names go on and on—Pope Leo, Bad Bill, Big Yellow, Three-finger John. If they hadn't brought a nickname with them when they came here, they usually acquired one in here. . . . " His voice trailed off and he stared wistfully into space.

Moved by the depth of feeling Captain Rankin had expressed for these long-dead men, Trout had a startling insight. Could it be that this empathetic keeper looked upon these men whose needs he tended during their final hours—these ghosts from the past—as family?

Captain Rankin cleared his throat. "Where was I? Oh, yes. Details. The oldest was sixty-seven, the youngest sixteen. In all, only three were over fifty. Ten were in their teens. The rest fall in between.

"The most to go in a single night was seven. They had all exhausted appeals and the governor—Flem Sampson, it was—sent down word to clean house. Kentucky took a lot of criticism for that night of carnage, from all around the country. That's a nationwide record, by the way—still stands."

Trout underscored the word carnage in his notes.

"What else?" Captain Rankin said. "Oh, yes, the crimes. A hundred and fourteen were executed for murder, nine for rape, one for armed robbery. Now, have I forgotten anything?"

Trout folded his note pad. "Captain Rankin, may I see the electric chair?"

The captain led him first to the dynamo room just off the death chamber. "We call this the control station."

The rubber-carpeted room housed a General Electric generator, a control panel, and a wall-mounted mesh of copper wires. Captain Rankin explained: "A half-hour before midnight the engineer comes down and starts the dynamo. The current builds up in the dummy load—that mesh of wires over there. The engineer stabilizes it at twenty-three hundred volts. This small window here gives him a view of the death chamber. When the warden gives the signal, the engineer throws this switch here, sending the current from the dummy load to the chair. One shock—twenty-five seconds—is usually all it takes. But I've seen it take eight."

"Eight!" Trout exclaimed. "You mean eight *separate* shocks?"

"If the physician says the man isn't dead, it's the only thing to do."

In the main corridor, Captain Rankin opened the green-and-tan door and bade Trout to enter. Trout's eyes riveted on the lethal instrument near the back of the room. He had seen the electric chair before. Nonetheless, the sight caused a cold tremor up his spine.

Captain Rankin patted the high back of the chair. "This is 'Old Lightening Bolt,' 'Blue Streak,' 'Sparky,' 'The Widow Maker'—it goes by a lot of names. Would you like to sit in it?"

"No, thank you," Trout said, giving his head an emphatic shake.

"You'd be surprised how many visitors do that," the captain said.

A table against one wall bore a tub of water in which several items were soaking. Nearby lay a football-like helmet. Captain

Rankin withdrew a four-inch copper rod from the tub. It had a small copper plate welded to one end. A sponge was pushed down over the rod, resting against the plate. "This is the electrode for the head. It's been soaking in salt water since noon. The sponge makes for a better electrical connection."

He picked up the helmet. There was a small hole in the crown. "The rod screws through this hole, pressing the plate against the man's head, a shaved spot"—he touched the back of his head—"here, at the base of the skull. The other electrode, soaking in the tub there, fits on the leg. When the switch is thrown the current flows from head to leg. The brain dies first."

He replaced the electrode back in the saline bath. "Any questions, Allan?"

Trout thought of what he'd heard. Captain Rankin had certainly provided details. Trout had listened in awe, even fascination, to some of the things the man had related, but he also felt a sense of foreboding. He projected his thoughts eight hours ahead, to what would occur in this room shortly after midnight.

He said, "Captain, I'd like to talk to the condemned men."

"Like the warden said, that's up to them," Captain Rankin replied. "I'll leave you alone in the corridor. I'll be in my office if you need me."

Tom Penney was sitting at his desk, engrossed in something he was writing. He shoved the paper into his desk drawer when Trout approached.

"Tom, I'm Allan Trout, with *The Courier-Journal*."

"I've read your column for many years, Mister Trout."

Tom listened politely while Trout explained the reason for his visit—an in-depth feature for a future column, not tomorrow's headlines.

"Mister Penney, is there anything you would like to say to my readers?"

"I have taken a vow to say nothing more about the case, Mister Trout."

"A personal question then. I knew Marion Miley. I spent an afternoon with her in Lexington just before . . . she died. I understand your job required you to deliver beer to the country club. I wonder if you ever met Marion? Before that night, I mean. Do you ever think of her?"

Penney's expression chilled and Trout steeled himself for the invective he expected to come. Instead, speaking slowly, as if the words pained him, Tom said, "I never knew her, I never saw her that I know of before that night. I think of her constantly."

He turned back to his desk, and Trout knew the interview was over.

Trout went to the middle cell. During the reading of the warrant, Willie Baxter's sallow face had been masked in a complaisant smile. Now, as Trout explained his purpose, it was the same. It disturbed the reporter. Then he recognized it for what it was—the countenance of a man who was afraid to offend. How ironic. Should he question Willie at all? His part in the crime had been so peripheral. He had never been good copy. The drama of the story lay elsewhere. Yet there was something that puzzled Trout. "Mister Baxter, I've researched all the news articles about you. Variously, I've found you referred to as 'Ray' or 'Raymond.' The only nickname I've ever seen in print is 'Skeeter,' never 'Willie.' Where did you pick up the name 'Willie'?"

The little man emitted a squeaky laugh. "From a teacher, when I was a kid. I wasn't no good with books and things and she said it was because I didn't care none. She used to make me stand up in front of the class and told the other kids to laugh at me. Told 'em not to ever be like me, 'cause I was just 'willy-nilly' about things. I didn't even know what it meant, but the other kids started calling me that, then just Willie. After that, some folks called me that, and some folks called me Skeeter. Didn't make no difference to me. Then when I got put in here, Archie, he wouldn't call me anything else but Willie. He's in the next cell. Well, he *was*, 'cept they moved him this morning so's he won't be in the way tonight. He jokes a lot, see. Anyway, he says I remind him of a guy in a song they sing here about a death house con called 'Poor Willie.' That's what Archie calls me—'Poor Willie.' Don't bother me none, tho'."

In addition to everything else, the little man had lost his

name. Trout said, "Mister Baxter, is there anything you would like to say to my readers?"

Willie's brow furrowed for a few seconds, then his face clouded. "Tell 'em I'm awful sorry."

Bob Anderson was standing at the bars of his cell when Trout approached. "I've been listening," he said. "I don't want any questions, but here's your quote. Put it big black letters so the sons of bitches can't miss it: *As God is my witness, I am innocent of this crime!*"

He turned his back.

Trout sat in Captain Rankin's office, reviewing his notes. He was grateful to the death house supervisor—this gold mine of information—and told him so.

His mind kept replaying Bob Anderson's volunteered quote. He got another cup of coffee from the captain's pot, then asked, "Captain Rankin, you've witnessed all hundred and twenty-four executions, right?"

"Every one."

"Tell me, how many men maintained their innocence right up until the end?"

"Right up until the end?" Captain Rankin repeated. "Only one."

Only one, Trout thought. He would have to get the captain to tell him that story, too. But right now his mind was on Bob Anderson: *As God is my witness, I am innocent of this crime!*

What if Anderson repeated that ringing declaration tonight in the electric chair? The law was clear. Warden Buchanan would have no choice but to proceed with the execution.

And it would devastate him.

17

Just outside the village of Kuttawa, two miles northwest of Eddyville, a gravel spur road led to a high ridge overlooking the Cumberland River. There, situated at the edge of a long-neglected town park, a vine-covered arbor commanded a view of the Cumberland River for miles in each direction. From here one could watch fishermen run trotlines from bank to bank between swirling eddies, wave to boat pilots threading oil-laden barges between channel markers, and mark the progress of farmers just beyond the far bank preparing the rich bottom lands for spring crops. It was one of the few places along the river where the penitentiary that dominated the skyline from all other directions could not be seen. Years before, Warden Buchanan had found the deserted park to be a tranquil oasis in an otherwise turbulent world.

As he took a seat on one of the arbor benches this late afternoon, the out-of-sight institution he sometimes came here to elude was very much on the warden's mind. He had informed Deputy Warden Lady where he would be. He knew that Lady could send Macon Talbot for him, but would do so only if it became absolutely necessary.

He studied the peaceful scenes of the valley for a moment, then slipped on his glasses and pulled Allan Trout's rough draft of "To Kill or Not to Kill" from his pocket. He read:

> The practice of capital punishment is rooted in the ancient tribal custom of placating the gods with human sacrifices. Every organized society in recorded history has inflicted capital punishment in one way or another. In the United States, in order of preference, the instruments of death are electrocution, hanging, lethal gas, and shooting.
>
> Historically, the death sentence has been administered for a variety of offenses, including murder, rape, kidnapping, armed robbery, burglary, theft, and vagrancy. English history records the hanging of a ten-year-old boy for stealing a few lumps of coal. New Mexico archives record the execution of a man who was hung "for just being a damned nuisance."
>
> In Kentucky, capital punishment was originally administered by hangings, often reaching the fervor of a Roman Holiday. Spectators jostled for a good view. Families reserved choice seats for their children. Picnic lunches were spread in the shadow of the scaffold where vendors hawked souvenir programs. On one occasion, a condemned man and his rape victim were permitted to engage in a lengthy and acrimonious argument, to the delight of some of the onlookers, before the trap was sprung. Mounting revulsion over these spectacles prompted abolition of public executions and the rope. Since 1920, all legal executions

in the state have been carried out in the electric chair
in Eddyville. . . .

"In Eddyville," the warden repeated in his mind.

There was more to Trout's column, but the warden didn't
want to read it now. He put the draft back in his pocket.

He had witnessed the "spectacles" Trout wrote about, many
times. *Justice*, he preferred to call them—at one time. He'd been a
lawman all his adult life—a hard-nosed, "hang-'em-high"
proponent of legal execution. But now . . .

But now, what? Why had the hint of disclaimer even
entered his mind?

He thought about Tom Logan, the warden he had replaced,
the warden who refused to attend a single execution during his
tenure, delegating what he held to be an odious duty to deputies
instead. It was Logan who told Buchanan the chilling story of
Ted Black.

One summer night years before, police on routine patrol
through a Louisville park found Black and his girlfriend lying on
the ground beside his car in a remote wooded area. Black was
passed out drunk. The girl, partially disrobed, was dead. She had
been raped, then beaten to death with a large boulder found
nearby.

Brought to trial for murder, Black testified that he and the
girl had gone to the park to make love. He said he had passed out
while his girlfriend was disrobing and didn't remember anything
after that.

The state's star witness was a high school girl who claimed
to have been riding her bicycle through the park that evening and
had seen everything from a nearby hill. Black, she testified, had
beaten the dead girl with the rock, then passed out just before the
police car arrived. Based on this eyewitness testimony, Ted Black
was convicted and sentenced to death.

During the trial, one person became skeptical of the young
girl's testimony—her mother. The story the girl told from the
witness box didn't ring true to the mother then, nor did it
afterward when she repeated the story to reporters. The mother's

attempt to question her daughter triggered anger and defiance. One week after the trial, the daughter left home and moved in with her boyfriend.

For months there was no contact. Then, late on the night Ted Black was scheduled to be executed, the daughter appeared at her mother's door in tears. She had perjured herself, the distraught girl admitted. Between contrite sobs, she blurted out the story. She *had* been in the park that evening, but she had seen two men at the scene of the murder, not one. Ted Black was passed out on the ground. The second man was running from the scene. He spotted her standing beside her bicycle on the hill and came to her.

"Did you see what happened?" he asked.

"Uh-uh," the girl replied. "I just got here."

At that moment they saw a patrol car enter the park though a distant gate.

The fleeing man said, "Well, that guy lying down there on the ground just beat that girl with a rock." He took out his wallet and handed the girl twenty dollars. "Tell the police that's what you saw. Then buy yourself the prettiest dress in town."

When he handed her the money, the girl told her mother, she saw that his hands were bloody.

Mother was horrified. "My God! Why did you agree to such a terrible thing?"

"Because," the girl sobbed, "I wanted the dress."

The papers that morning reported that Ted Black was to be executed shortly after midnight. The mother looked at the clock: 1:00 A.M. Her heart sunk. Then she remembered—Eddyville was in the Central Time Zone. That meant it was only midnight there.

Frantic, she wondered whom to call. She doubted she could get through to the governor. The prosecutor! He was a well-known Louisville attorney. She looked up the number and dialed.

Ted Black was strapped in the chair when the phone in the death house supervisors office began to jangle. The governor was on the line.

Ted Black was saved from execution, within seconds of death.

Now, on the bench overlooking the Cumberland, Warden Buchanan mulled the incident over. Such a case was an anomaly, a rare slip-up in a well-ordered legal system.

"Damn!" he said aloud.

Rare slip-up? He knew better. He was a board member of the American Prison Congress. He had served as vice president of the organization. He knew and associated with wardens and other respected penologists from all parts of the country. He had never met a warden from a capital punishment state who was without a private horror story about the execution of an innocent man. Not one.

His thoughts turned to Bob Anderson. That was the crux of the matter, wasn't it? The gut fear that Anderson could be another Ted Black, but that in this case, the witness against him might not recant. He dreaded the thought of learning someday that Tom Penney had indeed hoodwinked them all and railroaded the nightclub owner for personal revenge.

He thought back over his years as warden to the men whose executions he had supervised. He was surprised how clearly he could recall them. No, not surprised, really. They were always there, filed in some permanent niche in his brain, ever waiting to be called to mind. Though they rarely spoke of it, it was the same with other prison officials he knew. Indeed, he had been compelled to release from duty guards to whom such persistent memories had become debilitating nightmares.

One of the first executions he had supervised was a mere lad of seventeen. There was a bitter memory about the incident. As the warden and others were filing out of the death house after it was over, the prosecuting attorney, down from Louisville to witness the execution, remarked, not without pride, "Jess, if I'd been defending that boy instead of prosecuting him, he'd have gotten off with ten years."

He hadn't slept well that night.

Willie Baxter's pathetic countenance took shape in his mind. Could the same be said for Willie? Could the state's venerable prosecuting attorney in the Miley case have gotten the pitiable little man off with a lesser sentence had he defended rather than prosecuted? The warden and the prosecutor were good friends, but the warden knew he would never ask.

Then there was this recent invitation to meet with Senator McKellar to discuss the penal reform bill. Senator Barkley had recommended him for that. At a Jackson Day dinner in Louisville some years before, the warden and Barkley had gotten into a discussion about capital punishment. "Jess," Barkley asked at one point, "how many affluent men have been executed at Eddyville?"

"None," the warden admitted.

"And there won't be. We reserve the extreme penalty for those without influence, defendants who can't afford the Clarence Darrows." Then the esteemed senator added a declaration that haunted the warden at every execution thereafter. "Only the helpless hang, Jess."

Only the helpless hang.

Is that what it came down to? A life-or-death battle of wits to determine who had the most competent lawyer? Or the most expensive?

What about the alternative practiced in some states: Life without mercy—a true life sentence without the opportunity of parole? Would that satisfy the hard-liners who cried for blood—for absolute vengeance? He doubted it.

He thought of the thugs he'd dealt with as a lawman—scum who would slice your guts open just to hear you scream. Did they deserve to live? Didn't the state have a right to exact the extreme sacrifice from such animals?

The state.

There was the problem. It was not some nebulous entity called the state that executed men. It was *men* who executed men, and often paid a fearful price for it.

18

On previous occasions when Allan Trout visited Eddyville, he had been invited to join the Buchanan family for dinner in the palatial dining room in the rear of the warden's apartment. Often, he was an overnight guest. On this occasion, although the invitation had been extended, Trout declined. He knew that the warden had too much on his mind to be bothered with entertaining guests.

Instead, Trout took dinner in the reporters room with his colleagues. It was meat day at the prison, and the meal that evening was stew made from beef and vegetables, both raised and processed on the prison farms. Trout was not much of a red meat eater. His main reason for eating at the prison rather than going to one of the cafes in town was so that he could enjoy once again the crusty, prison-baked bread. Freshly prepared each day from a simple white-flour recipe, it was a true delicacy relished by every person who tasted it, convicts included. Trout had first eaten the bread at the warden's table. Thereafter, he often took a loaf or two home with him, tipping the prison bakers generously for the privilege. Since he planned to leave Eddyville that night, he would have to forego that booty this trip.

Midway through the meal that afternoon, the discordant clang of a not-too-distant bell rang out loudly. Veteran reporters who had covered events at Eddyville before kept eating. First-timers looked up in alarm.

"What's that?!"

"That's the OK bell," Trout explained. "The guard captain rings it every evening after cellblock count. It means all the inmates are present or accounted for and the lock-down for the night is complete."

The newcomers gave a sigh of relief and returned to their meals.

After dinner, Trout decided to escape the institution for a while. Following his visit to the death house that afternoon—after the well-spent time with Captain Rankin—he had much to assimilate with the previous research he'd done on the practice of capital punishment. He decided to take a drive to think things through.

The heart of Eddyville lay in a single three-block-long section at the bottom of the hill. Trout had collected data for a story on the river town a couple of years earlier and recognized the pertinent features. There was Rose Hill, ancestral estate of the Cobb family, which had produced the famed writer-humorist Irvin S. Cobb; Gresham Brothers Grocery Store, which held a flood sale every spring, come hell or high water; Charlie Clark's Poolroom, known for the best chili in Kentucky, which wasn't overstating it too much; and The Kentucky Theater, the only movie house in the county, where the owner, L. B. Fuquay, sometimes put on special matinees for prison trustees. Further on was the William Kelly House, where the inventor of steel had lived as a young man; then the remnant of what had been a fine turn-of-the-century hotel, where the Swedish Nightingale, Jenny

Lind, traveling by river steamer on tour for P. T. Barnum, had serenaded the populace during an overnight stop. Barnum had nearly succumbed to apoplexy on learning that she had staged the show for free.

The sights and memories of Eddyville were a momentary diversion for Trout, but not germane to his purpose. Just past the Turnaround Cafe, jumping this night with teenagers and home-on-leave GIs jitterbugging to a blaring jukebox tune, he turned his thoughts to a more relevant memory . . .

Allan Trout had begun to research the subject of capital punishment in earnest soon after an incident that occurred during what had started out to be a routine assignment. He had driven over from Frankfort to the University of Louisville to interview Dr. David Maurier, a professor of humanities in the English department. Professor Maurier had conducted years of research into white-collar criminal activities and was a noted authority on con men and their various ruses.

On campus that morning, Trout entered the anteroom outside Maurier's office in Gardner Hall to overhear the professor, on the other side of the open office door, in what sounded like heated debate with another person.

Embarrassed, Trout turned to leave.

He had just stepped back into the hallway when Professor Maurier caught up with him. "Allan. I thought I heard someone out here. Come back, please."

The professor led Trout back to the office and invited him to take a chair at the maple conference table where the debaters had been drinking coffee and holding forth. "Join us, please," Maurier insisted. "You just may find this interesting."

Professor Maurier made the introductions. Trout had never met the other man in the room, but recognized him as a noted jurist and faculty member of the University of Louisville Law School.

Professor Maurier poured coffee for Trout. "I suppose you overheard the subject of our discussion when you came in."

"No, not really," Trout replied.

"Oh? Then permit me to enlist you in the debate. May I ask, Allan, what is your opinion of capital punishment?"

Caught off guard, Trout pondered the question. It wasn't on his agenda for discussion. Still, he recognized a colorful slant to his story. He replied. "Off hand, if I had to vote on the question today, I'd probably vote against it."

"Bravo," Professor Maurier exclaimed. "Spoken like a member of the enlightened generation."

"Horse hockey," the jurist retorted. "It is the premature judgment of one who has not seriously examined the issues. No offense, Mr. Trout, but honestly, have you truly given serious consideration to the matter?"

"No, not really," Trout admitted.

Professor Maurier came to his defense. "Don't let him patronize you, Allan. It doesn't take gray hair and a juris doctorate to qualify one to pass judgment on such a fundamental issue. I suspect that you have given the subject more thought than you realize. Just to bolster your faith, let me reiterate arguments supporting your stand."

Trout pulled out his pad. "May I take notes?"

"Please do."

"And record," the jurist interjected, "that I shall rebut."

"No doubt," Professor Maurier said.

Maurier concentrated on Trout. "First, capital punishment is atavistic, a death ritual held over from the dark ages. It has no place in a civilized society. It doesn't return life to the murdered or chastity to the raped. To speak of the death penalty as vengeance is at once narrow-minded, morbid, and barbaric. The premeditated execution of the killer for revenge is violence begetting violence. So-called legal slaying is no less repugnant than criminal slaying. Do you agree, so far?"

"I believe so," Trout replied. He could tell that this was not a new subject to the professor.

The jurist lit a cigar and remained quiet.

"Next," the professor said, "a most important point—there's not one shred of evidence that legal executions deter crime.

Murder is just as prevalent where capital punishment is applied as where it's outlawed. The threat of the hangman simply does not stop criminals bent on violence.

"Next, for those so inclined, there's the religious prohibition. 'Thou Shalt Not Kill' is just as binding today as when it first thundered across Sinai thirty-four centuries ago. But religiously inclined or not, the notion that human life is sacred is almost universal."

He shot the jurist a pointed look, then continued. "Finally, I realize full well that a majority of people in this country, Kentuckians not excepted, support capital punishment. And my distinguished friend here berates me for being a 'bleeding heart liberal' for opposing the practice. But what is so liberal, I ask you, about keeping a felon confined behind bars for the remainder of his life? Isn't that harsh enough punishment—revenge, if you will—for the most heinous crime? Many more-progressive states agree. And it could be incorporated here. No one who knows Warden Jesse Buchanan at Eddyville doubts that he could establish the proper penal system in Kentucky. That, by the way, was the essence of our debate when you arrived."

Professor Maurier sat back. "I rest my case."

Trout had inscribed every word in his particular shorthand technique. "It was quite impressive," he remarked.

The jurist nodded. "Impressive, yes. Convincing, no. Just keep that pad open, Mr. Trout."

He pulled an ashtray near and laid his cigar in it. "Let's examine each point. My liberal friend here despairs that capital punishment doesn't resurrect the slain or restore chastity to the ravaged. Pray, what punishment will? If enrolling the felon in Yale for a course in remedial manners would revive victims we would all opt for that solution, but the dead remain dead. Is it mere vengeance to demand that the killer pay the same price? No, it is *retribution*. Legal executions may be violent, but *they are violence earned*."

He paused to let the point sink in, then continued. "I disagree that legal executions are as repugnant as murder. How many murder victims are granted public hearings? How many victims are represented by counsel paid for by society? How many victims have their cases endlessly appealed, are granted stay after stay, are offered pastoral service and given ample time to repent? How many? None, I submit. Yet these are routine rights provided to their killers.

"My colleague claims executions do not deter crime. Hogwash. Not one executed killer has killed again. But paroled killers do, all too often.

"The death penalty isn't effective? Ask any criminal investigator how may cases he was able to solve with the mere threat of a death sentence. Ask how many accomplices have fallen over themselves to turn state's evidence to keep from facing the electric chair or the hangman's noose. Their answers will make you think twice before discarding such an effective law-enforcement tool. The sad fact is, there are persons in our society who can be held in check only by fear. And the ultimate fear is death."

"Look . . . ," Professor Maurier cut in.

The jurist raised a hand. "I gave you an interrupted floor, David."

"Sorry."

The jurist continued. "Now, for the sixth commandment, that favorite scripture of the abolitionists: 'Thou Shalt Not Kill.' A more enlightened translation of the original Arabic would be: 'Thou Shalt Not Commit Murder.' *Murder*, Mr. Trout, is indeed a criminal act. But *legal execution* in not murder. No more so than is causing the death of an enemy in war. And indeed, it is exactly that—*war*—that society is engaged in against these culprits."

He took a drag from his cigar and laid it back in the ashtray. "Now, as to my good friend David's final argument, lifetime incarceration. It has two inherent weaknesses. One, it lacks the element of dread that is a positive deterrent. Two, in our prevailing social climate, it cannot be made to work."

He leaned back, choosing his words with care. "David believes that our esteemed warden in Eddyville could establish a workable lifetime incarceration program. Now, no man stands ahead of me in admiration for Jess Buchanan. I have watched him grow in statue to become one of the most respected lawmen and penologists in the country. Nevertheless, the disheartening fact is he is the personification of the end of an era. Jess Buchanan will be the last King of the Hill at Eddyville. Ten years from now a man like him won't even be able to get a job as a guard in our penal institutions. Why? Because David and his fellow liberal arts educators are reshaping our society. 'Degree! Degree! Degree!' The battle cry of the anointed. I submit that the time is fast approaching when a self-educated, self-made man, no matter what his capability, won't stand a chance against the sheepskin holders. In many states, psychologists and social workers are already taking over the penal systems. Do you know that there is a move afoot in Frankfort right now to change the title *Warden* to *Superintendent*? Superintendent, for God's sake! What they have in boys schools.

"What does all this mean? It means that prisons will be run by consensus. The committees that Buchanan has banned at Eddyville will re-emerge when he departs. Shrinks will decide who gets trustee status, who gets paroled, who receives discipline, and in what manner. Can you foresee the result? I'll help you. The head-thumpers will be conned out of their skulls by hoods who learned more about human nature in the mean streets than any paper chaser could possibly learn in the halls of ivy. I submit that a life sentence will be meaningless. So-called rehabilitated killers will be released to prey again on society. I suggest, gentlemen, that we should do all in our power to avoid such a world for as long as possible."

He sat back. "So, the rebuttal rests."

A road sign just ahead interrupted Trout's reminiscence. He had driven miles further than he had intended. He pulled into a country lane, turned around, and started back toward Eddyville.

Recalling again those opposing arguments he had heard at the University of Louisville that day—and had dutifully recorded in his notebook—Trout thought again of the factor that the debaters had ignored. It was the factor that had haunted the Miley case ever since Tom Penney's contradictory testimonies about Robert Anderson hit the headlines, the factor Trout knew was causing Warden Buchanan and others concern on this execution eve.

The indisputable factor: wherever capital punishment is practiced, the potential of executing an innocent person is ever present.

19

The sun had just begun to set when Father Thomas Libs drove up to the ferry slip on the west bank of the Tennessee River. The ferry, visible in the twilight of the ending day, was unloading cars on the opposite bank and would remain there until enough westbound cars arrived to make the return trip profitable. Father Libs turned off the engine and settled back for a long wait. With a twinge of guilt, he realized he didn't mind the delay. He was not looking forward to what lay ahead this night.

Thirty-two-year-old Father Thomas Libs was the assistant curate at St. Francis De Sales Church in Paducah. It was his duty to drive once each month to Eddyville to celebrate Mass for the Catholic inmates at the penitentiary. Kentucky was not a stronghold of Catholicism, and the convict population reflected the fact. There were seldom more than fifty inmates, out of a population over twenty times that number, who professed the Roman faith. Still, the prison ministry was arduous and time-consuming. First, there was the trip itself. Paducah was only twenty-eight miles from Eddyville, but the towns were separated by two major rivers—the Cumberland and the Tennessee. The inevitable long delays at the two ferry crossings, plus the restrictive war-time speed limit, meant a minimum of three hours driving time for the fifty-six-mile round trip. Then there were the Mass, Holy Communion, confessions, and the myriad personal problems, real and fancied, of incarcerated men. All in all, with two large parishes in Paducah to attend, Father Libs seldom had enough time for his prison flock, and never enough time for extended ministering to any one inmate. It was a situation he regretted, and one that had caused serious problems with one well-publicized prisoner.

On the day Tom Penney was transferred from jail in Lexington to the death house at Eddyville, Church officials in Lexington wired an urgent request to Paducah for Father Libs to go at once to the prison to become acquainted with the new convert. Father Libs was astonished. Such a request was without precedent. Even if it were not, Father Libs had no time to spare from his demanding duties in Paducah to make a special trip to Eddyville solely to meet one newly arrived member of the congregation. He explained this to his bishop, with a promise that he would make it a special point to meet with Penney during the next regular visit to the prison. The bishop agreed that Father Libs' decision was reasonable.

Tom Penney did not.

For the past year in Lexington, in the glare of media spotlight, Penney had enjoyed a singularly devoted ministry from Father George Donnelly, who spent hours at the city jail instructing the new convert and answering the multitude of questions that burned in the heart and mind of the inquisitive convicted killer. After being transferred to Eddyville, Penney remained convinced that his special circumstance continued to warrant special attention. Father Libs disagreed. The young priest's attitude rankled the new convert.

When at last they met late one afternoon following Father Libs's regular services at the prison, Tom shoved a four-page written agenda through the bars and suggested they discuss each item that evening. Father Libs discerned the situation at once. Like many converts in the heady flush of new-found faith, Tom sought to monopolize the time of any priest who would indulge him. In Lexington, he had been indulged, but Father Libs would not—could not—devote what precious little time he had for Eddyville to the demands of one man.

The harried priest attempted to explain. "Tom, your request is unreasonable. Perhaps I could bring you some books. . . ."

Tom snatched the list from Father Libs's hands. "Forget it, Father!"

That night Tom wrote a bitter letter to Father Donnelly complaining that Father Libs was indifferent to him.

Early in the morning, the day after receiving Tom's letter, Father Donnelly cancelled his appointments in Lexington and made the long drive to Paducah. That evening in Father Libs's small, cluttered office at St. Francis De Sales, Father Donnelly got straight to the heart of the matter. He showed Father Libs Tom's letter. "The man is hungering for the Eucharist, Father. I realize that he's only one member of a particularly trying congregation, but he's the only Catholic on death row. Perhaps his case does warrant a little extra care."

Father Libs was impressed with the older priest's fervor, but not his argument. "Father Donnelly, with all respect may I ask, How many condemned men have you dealt with?"

Father Donnelly was taken aback. "Tom is the first."

Father Libs nodded. "Then you must forgive me for my next question—you see, a death house priest develops a certain skepticism. Father, are you convinced that Tom Penney is a sincere convert?"

So that was it. Father Donnelly was not angry with the question. He had witnessed insincerity many times himself, and certainly Father Libs must have come up against a frustrating amount of it at the prison. But the young priest was wrong about Tom.

"Father Libs," Father Donnelly replied, "I have never instructed a convert whom I consider to be more sincere."

It was said with a conviction that precluded further argument.

"Very well," Father Libs conceded. "I will accept your assurances. However, I'm afraid that special visits remain out of the question. I will, of course, visit Tom each month. And I'll make a special point to be there for his final Eucharist."

Although not fully satisfied, Father Donnelly acquiesced. "I'll explain things to Tom tonight."

The explanation fell on unreceptive ears. That night at Eddyville, Tom delivered an ultimatum. "Forgive me, Father Donnelly, but I simply cannot accept Father Libs as my spiritual advisor. Unless *you* are here to administer my final Eucharist, I will forego it."

Not a man to be bluffed in normal circumstances, Father Donnelly perceived that these circumstances were not normal. He had ushered Tom into the Faith. It was only reasonable that the repentant sinner would want his most trusted priest to continue to minister to him and to be with him on the night he went to the Lord.

"Very well, Tom. God willing, I will be here."

Once each week for the remainder of that year, with Father Libs's understanding and blessing, Father Donnelly made the gruelling five-hundred-mile round trip between Lexington and Eddyville to prepare Tom Penney for his final sacrament.

Then, a few days before Christmas, Tom startled the world with his announcement that Bob Anderson was innocent. The executions were put on hold.

Upon hearing the news, Father Donnelly, now in the uniform of an Army chaplain, went to the prison at once. "Tom," the priest said, "your announcement changes things. There are Catholic boys away at war and I'm determined to be with them. I can't wait for the outcome of new trials."

Although distraught, Tom said he understood.

They spent the remainder of the afternoon together in Tom's cell. When he rose to depart, Father Donnelly said, "It could well be that this is the last time you and I will meet in this life, Tom. If that's the case, I deeply regret that I won't be with you during your final hours. But Father Libs *can* be, and will be if you ask. It's up to you. I suggest you do that soon—and you might apologize to him at the same time."

With a final blessing, Father Donnelly left his famed convert for the last time.

As the days passed, Tom made no effort to contact either priest. Then, a week after his last meeting with Father Donnelly, he held a press conference to announce that he would say no more about the Miley case, ever.

The following month, the Lexington court denied Bob Anderson's request for a new trial because of Penney's refusal to cooperate. Late on the night that the convicted trio were returned to Eddyville from the aborted hearing in Lexington, Tom called Captain Rankin to his cell. Tom was standing at the bars, his countenance anguished. "Captain Rankin, please get a message to Father Libs just as soon as you can. I must talk to him . . . It's urgent."

Two days later Father Libs came to the death house. Tom was pacing the floor of his cell. At the sight of the priest he stopped and gripped the bars. "Father, you've heard about the new date?"

The court of appeals had announced the new execution date soon after the hearing in Lexington. "Yes, Tom," Father Libs replied. "Two weeks from now. The twenty-sixth."

"Father"—Tom's voice was strained, the arrogance of their earlier meeting was gone—"I've been gambling with my soul. I have committed an offense against you and against God. If you can forgive me, could you . . . would you . . . be with me that night? I . . . need you."

Although wary, Father Libs accepted Tom's newfound humility at face value. "Yes, Tom. I'll be here."

It was that promise that Father Libs was en route to keep as he waited this late afternoon at the ferry crossing.

It was almost a year to the day since he and Tom had experienced their first abortive meeting, and there were still things about the man that disturbed the priest. Not least was the unseemly fact that the convicted killer had become something of an obsession in Church circles, not just among laymen. Since Tom's widely heralded conversion in his Lexington jail cell, religious orders in at least six states had undertaken a year-long prayer vigil to assure that Tom Penney's soul would enter Heaven as cleansed of sin as any saint's. Indeed, according to church bulletins, on this execution eve, over eight thousand masses were being held around the country for the same purpose. Then, only the previous week, Libs had learned that the church had arranged for Tom's body to be interred in sacred ground. Certainly, the intent of those kneeling in prayer on behalf of the once-fallen man could not be faulted. Yet Father Libs could not help wondering how many of them would be so attracted to the cause if it were not for the notoriety of the convert and the enormity of his sin?

Also, the priest reflected, there was this confusing business with Bob Anderson. For what godly reason had Tom absolved Anderson, then refused to save the man's life by backing up the statement with testimony? Was there, Libs agonized, a monstrous injustice about to be committed at Eddyville this night?

Father Libs was not proud of his misgivings about Tom Penney. He feared they revealed more about himself than about the convict.

A harsh blast from a klaxon horn startled Father Libs. He glanced up, surprised to see that the ferry had crossed the river and was on-boarding cars on his side. The ferry master was waving him aboard. Father Libs started the engine and drove down the steep gravel embankment onto the flat, barge-like boat. He pulled forward to the chain barrier and locked the parking brake. Then he turned off the ignition key and tried to purge the nagging doubts from his mind. Whatever his private thoughts, there was a more serious matter to contemplate. There were souls in need at the prison this night, and he vowed to do his priestly best to minister to those needs.

◆　◆　◆

At that moment, twenty miles from where Father Libs was crossing the Tennessee River, the man who so occupied his thoughts was in turn thinking about the priest. As Tom Penney sat on his bed watching the last sullen dusk settle around the dwindling hours of his life, his mind was on Father Libs. They had reached a rapport of sorts, he and the young cleric from Paducah. Libs was no Father Donnelly, but he *was* an ordained priest. He could forgive sin, *any* sin. And he had promised to come early tonight. Good. That would leave plenty of time to enlist the unsuspecting Father in the last act, the final trump card that Tom Penney intended to play in this bizarre game of life and death.

The last meal arrived at 4:45 P.M.

Following a policy instituted by Warden Buchanan, the prison cooks had prepared enough food to last throughout the evening and feed everyone on death row, including Captain Rankin, the assigned guards, and those condemned men who had been moved to other cells on this occasion.

Captain Rankin set up a portable table in front of each of the cells where Bob, Tom, and Willie could reach it through the bars. After the first serving, he checked the trays. Bob had eaten sparingly; Willie's tray needed replenishing; Tom had not touched his food.

"Tom," the captain said, "you haven't eaten anything all day. Won't you try something? The chicken's mighty good, so's the steak. Is there something else you'd rather have me order for you?"

"No, everything's fine, Captain Rankin. I'll eat later. I just want to finish this letter first." Tom felt no need to explain to the captain that he was fasting until he had received his final host.

Captain Rankin picked up the tray. "I'll keep it warm until you're ready."

The captain stopped by the middle cell and picked up Willie's empty tray. He put Tom's food in the oven, then piled Willie's tray high with fried chicken, broiled steak, mashed potatoes, peas. He broke into a reminiscent smile when he added a couple of biscuits to the tray.

Once the kitchen had sent thirteen biscuits with a last meal. The condemned man wouldn't eat. "Thirteen's unlucky," he complained. He was serious.

Captain Rankin had counted out the biscuits, shoved the thirteenth into his mouth and chewed it down. "There. Everything's fine now. I ate the unlucky one."

Much relieved, the condemned man ate with gusto.

Anecdotes about last meals abounded, and Captain Rankin knew them all. One of his favorites concerned an elderly black man named Jess Sanders. For his final meal, Sanders requested his all-time favorite dish—baked possum. The kitchen staff was in a quandary. No one had the slightest idea where to find a possum, much less how to cook one. Captain Rankin took the problem to Warden Buchanan.

The warden, too, relished baked possum. He had often gone on late-night hunts for the animal with a friend who owned a large wooded farm near Princeton, twelve miles from Eddyville. The man lived in the back country and had no phone. Warden Buchanan had Macon Talbot drive him to the farm. Sure enough, the man had three young possums in fattening cages gorging on ripe apples and persimmons. The warden purchased the choicest of the lot. He returned to his apartment, dressed the animal out, and baked it himself, adding the obligatory sweet yams and apples to the same pan. The condemned man declared it the best he had ever eaten.

The entry buzzer sounded.

Captain Rankin carried the refilled food tray to Willie's

table then went to open the gate. Deputy Warden Lady entered, accompanied by Father Thomas Libs.

Deputy Lady spoke to the two husky guards seated just outside Captain Rankin's office. The two men had reported to the death house when the last meal arrived. In the history of executions at Eddyville only one condemned man had resisted. He splintered his chair against the floor and armed himself with two of the splintered legs. In the fierce battle that followed, he broke one guard's arm and struck Captain Rankin above the eye, creating a deep cut, before he was subdued. He was dragged to the electric chair, strapped in, and executed, struggling and cursing until the end.

The odds against such an incident were high. Still, Captain Rankin would be required to open the death cells several times tonight, and the two club-armed guards would be at his side each time.

The deputy warden handed a flat-folded cardboard box through the bars to each of the condemned men. He instructed them to pack their personal belongings to be mailed to their next of kin.

Father Libs went straight to Tom's cell. Tom was licking the flap of an envelope. "Tom, I'm sorry Father Donnelly couldn't be here with you tonight."

Tom shoved the sealed envelope under his pillow. "So am I."

Father Libs noted the empty food table. "You've been fasting?"

"All day."

"May I have the wafer, please."

Tom took the thin disk of bread from his desk drawer and handed it through the bars. Father Libs cupped it gently in his hands and carried it to Captain Rankin's office to transubstantiate.

Minutes later, the priest emerged from the office. Captain Rankin, flanked by the two guards, opened Tom's cell. Father Libs entered and Captain Rankin re-locked the door. The priest arranged a makeshift altar beside the bed and lit two candles.

Tom Penney dropped to his knees. There, keeling on the barren floor of his death cell, the most famous Catholic convert in death house history received the viaticum.

Sacrament completed, Tom rose and called to Captain Rankin: "I can use some of that chicken now."

Father Libs sat on the bed and watched Tom eat his first meal of the day—the last meal of his life. Tom's hair had been freshly trimmed. A spot the size of a silver dollar had been shaved at the base of his crown. His right pants leg was split from cuff to knee.

Tom noticed the priest looking at the split pants. "Leg's been shaved, too," he said. "The barber came about an hour ago and did us in Captain Rankin's office." He rubbed his chin. "Didn't shave our faces. Said someone would do that . . . afterward."

Father Libs winced. He despised this duty, this unnatural ritual of preparing a healthy human for premature man-ordained death. He stood and called for Captain Rankin. "Tom, I'm going to have a word with Bob and Willie. I'll be back."

"Willie wants you to pray with him. I can't speak for Bob."

Since hearing his death warrant read that afternoon, Bob Anderson had remained supine on his bed, staring at the ceiling. He had risen only twice: once to get a piece of chicken and a biscuit from his food tray, and once to take the cardboard box Deputy Lady pushed through the bars. He didn't respond when Father Libs called his name.

Father Libs persisted. "Bob, this is no way to prepare yourself for eternity. I want to help you."

Bob rolled half-over on the bed and fixed the priest with an icy stare. "Pardon my French, Libs, but *bullshit!* You want to help me? Talk some sense into that asshole 'convert' who's got you and the rest of the fatheads around here conned. Go do that and leave me the hell alone."

Father Libs lowered his head and prayed silently for the recalcitrant convict.

At the middle cell, Willie was tossing things into a cardboard box. Father Libs noted a wadded shirt, some socks, a half-depleted carton of cigarettes, and what appeared to be a number of comic books. "You look busy, Willie."

Willie stubbed out a cigarette on the bars. "Mister Lady says they'll send all this stuff home for us."

"Yes, they will."

"Hey, Father . . . can I ask you somethin'?"

"Anything, Willie."

Willie rummaged through the box and pulled out a well-thumbed pamphlet: "Father Smith Instructs Jones."

"Tom gave me it." He flipped through the pamphlet until he found what he was looking for. "Here. What's a ag— . . . ag— . . . "—he pointed with a nicotine-stained finger—"this word right here."

"Agnostic," Father Libs read aloud. "An agnostic is—"

Tom's voice cut in from the end cell. "An agnostic, Willie, is an atheist who's afraid to admit it."

Father Libs chuckled.

Willie stared, puzzled. "What's a atheist?"

Father Libs explained. "An atheist is a person who denies the existence of God."

The idea perplexed Willie. "No God?"

"Atheists seem to have convinced themselves that man is the highest form of intelligence, a most horrid proposal at best. I sincerely pray that there are no atheists here tonight."

"Yeah," Willie agreed. "Me too."

He tossed the pamphlet back into the box. "I don't know who's gonna get all this stuff."

"It will go to whomever you desire," Father Libs explained. "Who's listed as next of kin on your records?"

Willie shrugged. "I dunno."

How pitiful. Father Libs made a mental note to check Willie's records. "Willie, do you have anyone back home you'd like me to write to?"

"I had a girl once. I liked her a lot. We broke off, though, after . . . when I got sent up. She's forgot me by now. Naw . . . I ain't got no one."

"Tom says you would like for me to pray with you. Do you

know any prayers?"

Willie's brow furrowed. "I use'ta know one."

He bowed his head. "Now I lay me down to sleep./ I pray to the Lord . . . uh . . . I pray for the Lord, for my soul to keep./ If I should die before I . . . uh . . . wake up, / I pray . . . uh . . . for him to take my soul."

Willie looked up beaming. He had recited the fractured childhood prayer with deep feeling, as if it were the most meaningful scripture in his life.

If Father Libs was taken aback he gave no indication of it. "Very good, Willie. Now, I'd like to teach you something from the Holy Bible. Will you let me do that?"

"Yeah . . . sure. But I ain't got one."

"That's all right. You don't need one for this."

For the next half-hour Father Libs tutored Willie in the words and meaning of the Twenty-Third Psalm. "Now, Willie, here are the words I want you to hold onto tonight: *Yea, though I walk through the valley of the shadow of death, I will fear no evil; for Thou art with me . . . and I will dwell in the house of the Lord forever. . . .'"*

Father Libs asked, "Do you understand what those words mean?"

"They mean I ain't to worry none, 'cause if I believe in the Lord, and I'm really sorry for what I done, like I am, then I'm gonna go to Heaven."

Father Libs was touched. No priest could have expressed it more meaningfully. "Excellent, Willie. Exactly right. Now, let's say them together until you know them by heart."

The entry buzzer sounded.

Father Libs glanced up to see Reverend Chandler, the Methodist minister who was full-time chaplain at the prison, enter the death house. It was the reverend's third visit to the condemned men this day, and this time he would remain until the end.

A graying, moon-faced man of beefy build, Chandler had been assigned to the prison ministry for five years. In addition to his duties as chaplain, he was also Director of Education at the institution. The first day on his new job he approached Warden Buchanan. "Warden, I wonder if you could recommend some good books on criminology and penal reform that I could study?"

Warden Buchanan replied, "Reverend, there are fifteen hundred crime books walking around inside these walls. I suggest you study *them*."

Study them he did. In the ensuing years Reverend Chandler became one of the most sought-after counselors at the prison and a person the inmates knew they could trust.

On entering the death house this evening, the reverend went first to Willie's cell. He greeted Father Libs, then Willie. "Looks like some mighty deep discussion underway here."

Father Libs explained that he had taught Willie part of the Twenty-Third Psalm. Reverend Chandler nodded approvingly.

"I'm afraid I can't reach Bob, though," Libs lamented. The priest explained what had happened when he tried to talk to Anderson.

"Oh?"

Reverend Chandler went to the first cell and called Bob's name. To Father Libs's surprise, Bob came to the bars and shook hands with the reverend, then the two entered into what appeared to be a serious discussion. Father Libs offered a silent prayer that the Protestant minister might succeed where he had failed.

While the men of the cloth counseled the condemned men, the prison officers retreated to Captain Rankin's office. As much as possible, prison officials kept out of a condemned man's last hours until the final minutes. Only if asked would an official keep a man company, and more than once Captain Rankin had played checkers or cards with a condemned man right up until minutes before he made the walk to the electric chair.

A half-hour before midnight, Chief Engineer Earl Chilton and three other men entered the death house. Two of the men entered the death chamber. Chilton and his assistant walked straight down the corridor to the control room housing the dynamo. They studiously avoided eye contact with the condemned men.

The two guards who entered the death chamber removed the electrodes from the saline bath. One picked up the helmet and screwed the larger electrode through the hole in the top until the soggy sponge and copper plate rested firmly against the inside liner. Then he stepped behind the electric chair and attached the exposed end of the electrode to a heavy black wire. He snapped a black hood in place on the front of the helmet and hung the helmet on the back of the chair.

The second guard attached the smaller sponge-backed electrode to straps at the chair's right leg. When he finished, he stepped to the small window between the death chamber and the control room and rapped. The window slid open.

"All set," the guard said.

"Stand aside," the engineer said.

Moments later the whine of the revving dynamo filled the death house, rose in pitch, then settled into a steady pulsating hum.

The sound of the dynamo galvanized the death house. Bob and Willie walked to the front of their cells and stared at the green-and-tan door. Tom bowed his head over his rosary. Deputy Warden Lady, Captain Rankin, and the two attendant guards took up stations to await the arrival of the warden.

Father Libs went to Willie's cell. Willie was standing with his hands gripping the bars, his eyes fixed on the door across the corridor. Father Libs said, "I'm going to be with Tom now, Willie, but I'll be with you also, in prayer. Remember the words we said together. Say them now. Repeat them when you step across the corridor. I'll be there, too."

Bob Anderson was barely listening to the prayer Reverend Chandler was reciting before his cell. How quickly it had all turned to ashes, Bob thought. When this day began he was positive that by now he and his lawyers would be mapping out his final irrefutable bid for freedom. Now, he had less than thirty minutes to live.

Captain Rankin let Father Libs into Tom's cell. Tom was kneeling beside his bed, head bowed, praying the rosary. Father Libs knelt beside Tom and prayed silently.

After a moment Tom raised his head and looked squarely into the priest's eyes. "Father, there's something you must do for me. On faith. No questions asked."

Tom reached beneath the pillow and withdrew the envelope he'd secreted there barely an hour before. It was sealed. It bore no name or address. He pressed the envelope into Father Libs's hands.

Father Libs's heart sank. Tom wanted him to smuggle a letter out of the prison, past the officials. He would not do that. He rose and held the letter out to Tom. "Tom . . . I can't be a party to—"

Tom grasped the priest's hand and folded it around the letter. "Father, I want you to give this letter to Warden Buchanan. But only after Bob and I are both dead."

Pearl Smith pushed the night buzzer on the counter at Knoth's Hotel to summon the proprietor. Minutes later, an elderly man wearing a frayed cotton robe over heavy flannel pajamas appeared from his living quarters. Rubbing sleep from his eyes, he gave Pearl a puzzled look. "No place to go in this town this time of night, lady. You catchin' the night train, maybe?"

"Yes, I am."

"Only one taxi in town. Old Tater's sawing logs by now. Probably cost you more this late, but his number's stuck up over there by the pay phone."

"No, that won't be necessary. I'll walk."

"It's two miles to the Kuttawa depot, Ma'am."

"I know."

The man took the ten-dollar bill Pearl held out and put it in a drawer under the counter. "Have to charge you for a full day, you know."

"I understand."

He handed her five ones in change. She put the money in her purse and stepped outside. The darkened streets of Eddyville were deserted. There were no stars to be seen in the overcast sky. Chilled, she pulled her coat tighter around her and started walking up the long hill toward the prison.

At the top of the hill, the River View Inn was still open. She remembered overhearing the proprietor say that he intended to stay open for customers who might want service after "the big doings across the street." In the faint glow of light coming from the cafe, she looked at her watch. It was 11:35. The "big doings" would soon be underway.

Remembering the details of the map in her pocket, she walked on past the prison until she came to a private home set back from the street just beyond the last cellblock. The home belonged to the Gracie family, who owned the farm that bordered state property. A narrow unpaved lane ran between the farm and the prison within twenty feet of the massive limestone walls. She turned onto the lane. It had been recently packed with cinders, and walking was difficult.

Lights from the cellblock to her right cast a checkered pattern along the way. Up ahead, she saw the wall-tower guard watching her. She didn't care. She was on private property. Besides, she knew that the guard knew where she was going. He had seen people go there before.

Fifty yards up the lane from the main highway, where Cellblock Three adjoined the death house, an enormous oak tree dominated the back acreage of the Gracie Farm. Twenty-four feet in circumference at its base, the majestic oak had taken root a full generation before the American Revolution. By the time the wooded hillside over which it stood sentinel was cleared to make way for the prison, the tree was well into its second century. For the past twenty-three years the tree's extending canopy had sheltered a series of strange rituals. Its proximity to the death house made it a convenient locale where family members, or the merely curious, could vicariously share a condemned man's final moments. Not many people were so inclined. Still, over the past two decades, enough distraught parents, wives, siblings, and children had gathered at the site for a final spiritual farewell that the old oak had entered prison legend as the "Vigil Tree."

Pearl stood with her back against the rough trunk. The night was pitch black. A single light, shining from somewhere on the other side of the prison wall, reflected upward onto the high branches of the oak. Pearl moved slightly to one side to have a better view of the light. She knew, as did all who ventured here, that when the switch to the electric chair was thrown, that light would flicker and grow dim. She couldn't explain the technical reason for it—that at the moment the voltage was transferred from the dummy load to the chair the dynamo would surge, momentarily drawing power from the main prison generators—she knew only that it happened. She also knew from news reports that the light would dim twice, once for Bob Anderson and once for Tom Penney, before it dimmed a third time for Willie.

She waited. And remembered . . .

For the first two weeks following Willie Baxter's arrest in Lexington, he was in no condition to receive visitors. Deprived of his needles, he was locked in a padded cell where he suffered the agonizing hell of cold-turkey withdrawal from his daily fix of heroin. Alternately racked by paralyzing, sweat-drenching tremors and fits of bashing his head against the wall, he wailed for hours in uncharacteristic rage. Each day Pearl came to the jail on Short Street. Each day she was turned away. At last, a sympathetic jailer added her name to the visitors list.

From the fist visit she pleaded with Willie to fight. "You're innocent, Willie. You didn't do anything! Tom did. You were with me, I'll testify to that."

The ordeal of withdrawal had left Willie pale and thinner. From the other side of the visitor's table, he looked at Pearl through sunken eyes. "I ain't innocent, Pearl. She'd still be alive today 'cept for me. Her 'n' Miss Marion, too."

He wouldn't budge from that self-accessed guilt, nor would he listen to her criticism of Tom. "Tom's my friend. Whatever he done, he's my friend."

"He is *not* your friend, damn it! He used you, Willie. He lied to you. Then he ratted on you. What kind of friend would do that?"

Willie would have none of it. In ensuing weeks he proved he was serious by corroborating everything Tom told investigators.

On her fourth visit, Willie asked Pearl not to come to see him again.

She was shocked. "For God's sake, Willie, why?"

"We ain't got nothing goin' for us no more, Pearl. Tom, he says him and me . . . we're dead men."

"That's not true. Least not for you. If you'll only fight. I told you I'd stick by you to the end. I will, Willie. I swear it. I'll hire a lawyer. Just fight for yourself . . . for us. Please . . . *fight*." For the first time in years she began to cry.

He stood, thrust his hands in his pockets and studied his shoes. It was deja vu, the way she'd first seen him standing in the sawdust that night in the carnival tent after her act, downcast, dejected, so all alone. Voice barely audible, he said, "Please don't do that, Pearl. It ain't no use. This *is* the end."

He turned and left the visiting room and went back to his cell.

She followed the trial in the papers, hoping against hope that Willie would come to his senses, or that justice would prevail and find him innocent or at least less guilty and spare his life. She would wait for him then. No matter how many years it took, she would wait.

But it wasn't to be. Like Bob and Tom before him, Willie was sentenced to die for being an accomplice in the murder of Marion Miley and her mother.

A sudden muffled whine jarred Pearl from thoughts of the past. Gary, who had given her the map, had briefed her on what that sound meant. The death house dynamo was running.

Her breathing became quicker and she fixed her eyes on the single light that reflected upward from behind the prison wall. In a few minutes that telltale light would signal a somber message into the dark night.

22

No person felt the burden of impending duty that evening more keenly than Warden Buchanan. Following his temporary retreat to the arbor in Kuttawa, he had returned to the prison at sundown. He took a light supper in his apartment dining room with his family, then called his friend Tom Waller at his home in Paducah. As promised, the attorney had been waiting for the call. No, Waller told the warden, he could find no error in the Bob Anderson's trial record. Notwithstanding, Waller added, apologizing for being unable to ease the warden's burden, the lack of error in the records did not preclude the possibility that Tom Penney had indeed railroaded the Louisville saloon keeper.

The warden called his office number, downstairs. When Henry Sproule answered, the warden asked if a phone line had been reserved for the remainder of the evening between Eddyville and the governor's mansion in Frankfort. Assured that it had been, he instructed Sproule to call him at 8:00 P.M. Then he went down the long hallway to seek a few minutes respite from the burdens of his responsibilities. Often he napped sitting upright in his leather chair in the living room. On other occasions, particularly on the eve of an execution, he retreated to the room he entered now—the Blue Room.

His wife had designed the Blue Room for just that purpose. Soon after moving to Eddyville, Mrs. Buchanan had appropriated the largest room in the spacious apartment and made it over into an elegant parlor. The hardwood floor was covered with a deep-pile indigo rug. The walls were papered with hyacinth-shade, woven-textured wallpaper. The oversize blue satin sofa, matching chairs, mahogany endtables, circa-1890 lamps, and a full-scale reproduction of Gainsborough's "Blue Boy" mounted above the fireplace, complemented the rich decor. The only incongruous notes to the tranquil setting were two floor-to-ceiling barred windows, which nonetheless were effectively camouflaged behind heavy cerulean curtains. Of all the rooms in the apartment, the warden found the Blue Room the most relaxing. Now, on this trying evening, he stretched his huge frame out on the sofa that had been elongated to his specifications, and rested for the ordeal to come.

The wake-up call from Henry Sproule came precisely at 8:00. The warden washed his face with cold water, then went downstairs to his office. He spent the next two hours working on the accumulated papers on his desk.

At 10:30 he sent Sproule to ask Allan Trout to come to the warden's office. It had happened before, and Trout knew what was expected of him. In times of stress, the warden needed the company of a trusted friend.

Trout settled into a chair near the warden's desk. "Jess, I got a call from an irate holy-roller preacher up in Bardstown the other day. He says you're permitting conjugal visits between some of the outside trustees and their wives. He was powerful upset about it. Now, I wonder if any of that's true and if there's a story in it for my readers?"

The warden tamped some fresh Kentucky Club tobacco into his favorite briar pipe, lit it, and tossed the match into a nearby cuspidor. "You know damned well it's true," he drawled after the first puff. "And it's none of your readers' or that Bible thumper's damned business."

Trout chuckled. It was just this type of unrelated talk that seemed to put the warden at ease. Trout continued. "All right. No story in the preacher. How about Mr. Hoover? How are you two hitting it off these days?"

The warden puffed his cigar for a moment, without replying. Trout's question was reference to an incident that was still being debated in penology circles.

A popular radio program at the time was "Gangbusters!", a dramatization of notorious crimes depicting the malevolence of criminals as opposed to the selfless magnanimity of law enforcement officials. Reminiscent of the western movie genre, each episode played out an archetypal black-hat, white-hat confrontation. Understandably, it was FBI Director J. Edgar Hoover's favorite program. The show's most diligent booster, he was often lauded on the air and often recommended other law enforcement officials he believed should be so rewarded. A few months earlier, at Hoover's suggestion, the producers invited Warden Buchanan to appear as a guest to introduce a segment based on his climactic capture of a felon currently serving time in the Kentucky State Penitentiary. The warden refused. Not only that, in a written reply he blistered the producers and sponsors for capitalizing on the misfortunes of not only the criminals but their victims as well.

Of course, the letter got to Hoover. The head G-man was incensed. The once warm relationship between him and Jess Buchanan chilled overnight.

Now, to Trout's query, the warden replied. "Hoover runs his show, and I run mine."

It went like that, give and take, for over an hour. And as the evening progressed, Trout detected a growing detachment in the warden's manner, a distraction beyond the inevitable tenseness of an approaching execution. With insight that had taken him to the pinnacle of his profession, the veteran reporter sensed that something unusual was afoot this night. Jesse Buchanan knew something that he hadn't revealed, and it seemed to be gnawing at his insides. Trout decided not to pry.

In the outer office, Henry Sproule had stationed himself by the phone. From the governor down, officials and attorneys knew that a call to Eddyville after midnight Central Time would almost certainly be too late to halt an execution. Still, on this night of multiple executions, Sproule would remain by the phone until it was all over.

As the final hour of that long day began a minute-by-minute march toward midnight, Sproule busied himself with typing the warden's outgoing correspondence for tomorrow. Finally, at 11:45, he rose and knocked on the frame beside the warden's open door. "Sir, it's time."

Warden Buchanan consulted his pocket watch. The dynamo would be running at peak load now. "Thank you, Henry." He knocked the ash from his pipe, placed it back in its niche in the rack, then rose and put on his coat. "Allan, let's go brief your friends."

The reporters room was crowded. Men young and old, most of whom had arrived late in the evening, sat at the table reading, jotting down notes, or working crossword puzzles. Some stood in huddled conversations around the walls. There were no women. A hush fell over the room when the warden entered.

The warden stepped to the head of the table. Trout sat down nearby. The warden said, "Gentlemen, in a few minutes it will be my duty—"

At that moment a loud *clunk* sounded near the window. A metal whiskey flask, now empty, bounced once more and slid to a halt at the warden's feet. Simultaneously, the young reporter Trout had admonished slid out of his chair onto the floor, and lay there unmoving.

Two reporters nearest their fallen colleague picked him up and propped him back in his chair.

The warden stepped to the door and called for two guards. When they came, he had them confiscate the flask, then directed them to carry the comatose young man to the guards quarters and put him to bed. "I want to see him in my office at seven o'clock tomorrow morning."

Allan Trout shook his head. He had tried to warn the young man. He knew that the reporter would never cover another story at the prison as long as Jesse Buchanan was warden.

After the guards and their burden were gone, the warden continued: "As I was saying, in a few minutes it will be my duty to carry out writs of execution against three men. Some of you have covered executions before. You know what to expect. Some of you have not. And it's those reporters that I want to talk to for a moment.

"As I'm sure Allan has explained to you, an execution is not like covering a fatal traffic accident. That's an after-the-fact assignment. An execution is not after-the-fact. It's a real-time event to which you are an eyewitness. It's not the easiest thing to watch for the first time, or any other time for that matter. And tonight, there will be three of them. Now, if for any reason any of you doubt that you won't be able to cope with that, I'd like to ask you to withdraw now. It's better for everyone concerned for you to make that decision here than to disrupt things in the death house later—which has happened."

He waited. No one withdrew.

"Very well. Now, old hand or new, there are a few rules you must abide by. This I want understood without exception: From the moment you enter the death house until the executions are over, you will remain absolutely silent. You will walk straight past the cells into the death chamber. No questions, no attempts at last-minute interviews, no distractions that would prolong things. That would be cruel to those men, and to us. I'll take whatever questions you may have after the final execution.

"Usually, following an execution, we leave the death house before the body is removed from the chair. We won't be able to do that tonight. If any of you have any qualms about that, come to grips with it now. It might help if you look away from the chair while the body is being unstrapped.

"Finally, if any of you begin to feel queazy, you will find

paper sacks under the chairs."

He looked around the room. "Any questions before we leave for the death house?"

There were none.

"Then it's time."

23

Bob Anderson was standing at the bars in front of his cell watching the clock above the green-and-tan door. Just as the large hand moved to one minute past midnight, Warden Buchanan and an entourage of officials and reporters entered the death house. The warden glanced at Bob, then turned to Captain Rankin. "Is everything ready?"

With those ominous words, Bob knew it was over. There had been no eleventh-hour call from the governor. The warden had not come to report a last-minute stay. He had come to carry out the sentence of the courts.

Captain Rankin replied, "Yes, Warden."

With military precision, Deputy Warden Lady herded the reporters, witnesses, and ministers through the green-and-tan door into the death chamber. Captain Rankin and his attendant guards followed and closed the door. As was his custom, the warden was alone in the corridor for a final private meeting with the condemned.

He went to the first cell. "Bob, do you have anything to say to me in private—in confidence, if you wish?"

Bob motioned toward the death chamber. "What I have to say I want all of them to hear."

The warden nodded. He put his hand through the bars and the two shook hands. "Goodbye, Bob."

Willie, too, was standing at the front of his cell. He had nothing to say in private. When they shook hands the warden noticed that Willie was trembling. He put his other hand atop Willie's and held it for several seconds. "Goodbye, Willie."

Tom was sitting on his bunk fingering his rosary. He got up and stepped forward when the warden approached. "Tom, Bob has about two minutes."

He waited.

Tom stood silent.

After a moment the warden extended his hand through the bars. "Goodbye, Tom." The two shook hands, then the warden turned and entered the death chamber.

He took his station three feet to the left of the electric chair and looked to make sure the window to the engineer's station was open. The engineer was watching him. The warden glanced around the room. Father Libs and Reverend Chandler were sitting on the front row. Allan Trout had taken a seat at the rear. The entire assembly waited in expectant silence.

The warden nodded to Captain Rankin.

Bob Anderson was lighting a cigarette when Captain Rankin and the two guards approached his cell. The captain unlocked the door. "It's time, son."

Bob flipped the match onto the floor and stepped into the corridor, flanked by the two guards. At the green-and-tan door he paused and looked toward the end cell. At the top of his voice he yelled, "TOM PENNEY, YOU MISERABLE SON OF A BITCH . . . I'LL BE WAITING FOR YOU IN HELL!"

The bold condemnation resounded through the death house.

Head high and cocky, cigarette dangling from his lips, Bob entered the pale green room and walked straight to the electric chair and sat down. With practiced haste, two guards buckled the wrist and leg straps in place, then tightened the chest strap over Bob's shoulders. One guard pushed the helmet down over Bob's head and took the cigarette from his mouth. Before the black hood was dropped, the warden asked. "Bob, do you have any last words?"

Bob looked boldly at the viewers. "Gentlemen . . . *I am innocent!*"

The warden winced. Of one hundred twenty-five condemned men to enter this chamber, Bob Anderson was only the second to proclaim innocence while strapped in the electric chair—and the first in Warden Buchanan's experience.

For the slightest moment, the warden hesitated. He glanced toward the chamber door. He had instructed Captain Rankin to leave it ajar, so that any sound, any cry from the corridor, might be heard. But there was only silence. For good or evil, Tom Penney had won the battle of wits. The warden nodded toward the engineer.

Reverend Chandler began to pray audibly.

There was a sudden change of pitch as the dynamo surged. Bob Anderson's body thrust forward with such force that had it not been for the restraining bonds it would have been propelled across the room. In horrid fascination, viewers watched as Bob's right hand opened and closed, slowly, like a mechanical claw, as it changed color from pink to mottled gray.

Twenty-five seconds later—an eternity to some viewers—the dynamo droned down to a steady whine. The prison physician stepped forward and placed a stethoscope on Bob's chest. After a moment, he nodded to the warden. Bob Anderson was dead.

A faint charnel odor permeated the death chamber. Some viewers placed handkerchiefs over their nostrils. Two convict corpsmen entered with a stretcher. When they removed Bob's body from the chair, his right leg, fused at the knee by the searing current, remained fixed at a 45-degree angle. The corpsmen placed a sheet over the body and removed it from the room.

Tom Penney entered the death chamber with his hands clasped behind his back and his head lowered. While the guards fastened the straps, Father Libs removed the crucifix he wore around his neck and held it high. Tom glued his eyes to the rood.

The helmet was put in place.

"Tom," the warden asked, "do you have any last words?"

Without moving his eyes from the cross, Tom replied, "Warden, I have told *you* the truth. Publish it."

At the rear of the room, Allan Trout sat forward on the edge of his seat. He had been right. The warden did know something that hadn't been told.

The warden said, "Tom, are you saying now that what you told me in December in confidence is the truth in this case, and that you want it told?"

Tom repeated cryptically, "I have told *you* the truth."

"That's your final statement."

"Yes sir."

The black hood was dropped in place and Father Libs began the prayer for the dying. Tom's body jumped against the straps, strained for twenty-five seconds, then relaxed. But this time the physician shook his head. Once again, Tom's body strained against his bonds, and once again the physician shook his head. Some of the viewers averted their eyes. Again, and yet again, Tom's body bore the crushing voltage.

Dear God, Father Libs prayed in fervored silence, *let this torment end!*

After the fourth shock, Tom Penney was pronounced dead.

The corpsmen entered to remove Tom's body.

From a middle row a reporter, unable to restrain his curiosity, stood. "Warden, what did he mean by—?"

The warden's steel-gray eyes flashed. Prudently, the reporter sat down.

Minutes later, Willie Baxter made his walk to death wearing the same meek smile he defensively projected throughout his life. As he passed Father Libs, the priest heard the squeaky voice: " . . .

through the valley . . . the shadow of death . . . "

After the strap-in the warden asked, "Willie, do you have any last words?"

Willie looked around the room, then at the warden. "I'm going home."

The next day that statement would be widely reported as Willie Baxter's final words. They were not.

Father Libs made the sign of the cross toward the frail little man. Behind the black hood, Willie whispered something that neither the priest nor the others could hear. Warden Buchanan, standing closer, heard it plainly. Willie Baxter's final word was: "Pearl."

At that moment, twenty yards on the other side of the steel-and-stone chamber where Willie was whispering her name for the last time, Pearl Smith kept her eyes riveted on the light that shone upward through the oak boughs. She had counted the shocks. One for Bob, then minutes of pause. Four in quick succession for Tom, then more minutes of pause. Now came the final, single dimming—for Willie. She wondered if she should pray. She'd never been religious and decided a prayer would be hypocritical. Nor would she cry. There had been tears enough following those painful days in Lexington when Willie had refused her pleas to fight, then kicked her out of his life. That was when he really died, she thought, when he accepted full blame for Mrs. Miley's death—*for Tom Penny's crime.*

Poor Willie, she thought. Poor simple, lonely, confused, vulnerable Willie. He had been her man, the only man out of thousands she had ever loved. She had promised him that heart-wrenching day in Lexington that she would stick with him to the end.

She had kept that promise.

She pushed away from the Vigil Tree and looked once again at the foreboding limestone wall behind which a cruel blood rite had just been enacted.

It was over.

"Goodbye, Willie," she whispered into the cold night.

It was thirty-three minutes past midnight.

24

The dynamo wound slowly down to a stop.

In the corridor outside the death chamber, reporters surrounded the warden, their voices a babble.

"What did he mean?"

"What did he say?"

"What did Penney tell you and no one else?"

The warden raised a hand. The crowd grew quiet.

The warden said, "A few days after Tom made his deposition absolving Bob of any involvement in the murders he asked to see me in private. We met in my office. He said he wanted to make a confession to me and me alone. He asked me if I would keep what he told me confidential until after he was dead. I agreed to do so, as long as it did not cause harm to another person. Then he told me that the deposition he'd made absolving

Bob was a lie. He said that Bob *was* his accomplice in the murders."

"But why? Why did he make a public issue of absolving Anderson, then recant? Did he explain?"

"He said only that he had been gambling with his soul. He told me that things would become clear at the end. Then he vowed to say no more about the case, ever. He kept that vow, I can assure you."

It didn't satisfy the questioners. "What did he mean about things would become clear at the end?"

The warden shook his head. "I have no idea. There's nothing more I can tell you."

The reporters hurried from the death house, anxious to get to phones. Allan Trout lingered behind. The irony of what had occurred during the past half-hour had not escaped him, and he realized it was news. But it could wait. When the corridor was clear he said, "Jess, Bob Anderson and Tom Penney just gave you two diametrically opposed death statements. Which do you believe is true?"

Trout could read the pain in the warden's reply, "Allan, I simply do not know."

Trout put his hand on the warden's shoulder for a moment, then left.

The doors to the death cells stood open, awaiting a cleaning crew that would prepare them for the next occupants. Alone in the corridor the warden studied the first cell, where Bob Anderson had spent the final months of his life. After a long moment, his mind deeply troubled, he turned to leave. He had reached the gate when a voice called, "Warden."

Startled, he turned to see someone step out from the death chamber.

"Father . . . I thought everyone had left."

"I waited until the others were gone," Father Libs replied. He reached into his coat pocket and withdrew an envelope. "Tom gave this to me during our final moments together. He asked me to deliver it to you personally, after he and Bob were both dead. I have no idea what it contains."

A tremor shot through the warden. Without a word he took the envelope from the priest's hand, stepped into Captain Rankin's office and closed the door.

25

The deserted highway, illuminated only by the headlights of Allan Trout's Chevrolet, wound like an ebony ribbon between the wooded hills. Trout drove slowly. There was still fifteen minutes before the 1:30 A.M. passenger train to Louisville would make its middle-of-the-night whistle stop at the Kuttawa depot, two miles away.

The freshman reporter he was taking to catch the train had just witnessed his first execution. "They just walked in and sat down," he remarked. "Almost casually. I don't understand it."

"Warden Buchanan has a theory about that," Trout said. "He believe's condemned men are dead before they get to the chair."

"Before?"

"In their minds," Trout explained. "He says once they

223

accept the inevitable, something prepares them for it. Psychologically, they kill themselves. There've been cases where condemned men cried in frustration when the warden told them they'd been granted a stay. It meant they'd have to go through getting ready for it mentally again."

"That's pretty damned interesting," the young reporter said. "I think I'll use that in my story."

"You won't be the first," Trout said.

Then he asked, "You have a berth tonight?"

"Yeah," the young man replied. "But I don't think I'll use it. I don't feel like being cooped up alone. I want to sit in a lounge chair among people. *Live* people. I'm sure I can find someone who'll trade a seat for a Pullman berth."

"I'm sure," Trout agreed, and understood.

"How about you?" the man asked. "You driving all the way back to Frankfort tonight?"

"I would, if it weren't for this tortoise-pace speed limit," Trout replied. "I've got a room reserved in Elizabethtown. I'll probably stop there for a few hours sleep."

At Mineral Mound Hill a sparse splattering of rain drops hit the windshield. Moments later, the car lights fell on someone walking on the side of the road. It was a woman. Trout pulled to a stop beside her. "You're going to get wet, Miss. Can I drop you off somewhere?"

"I'm going to the train station," Pearl Smith replied.

"So are we." Trout reached back and opened a rear door. "Hop in."

The mournful peal of a locomotive whistle sounded in the distance as Trout pulled into the depot parking lot. Except for a single high nightlight that dimly illuminated the loading platform, the small yellow frame building with the name KUTTAWA painted on it was dark. Pearl got out and pulled her yellow bandana tight to ward off the soft rain.

"Thanks," she said.

"You're welcome," Trout replied.

Pearl ran to the depot where she stood alone beneath a shelter at the end of the platform.

The young reporter said, "Now I remember where I saw that woman before. She was on the bus from Louisville this afternoon. I bet she's got someone doing time at the prison."

"Could be," Trout agreed.

A glaring headlight brightened the platform and parking lot as the giant locomotive rounded the final curve approaching Kuttawa station, then hissed to a stop in a cloud of steam. A porter jumped down from the lead passenger car, put a portable step on the platform, and helped Pearl aboard.

As the young man got out of the car, Trout said, "Since you're going to sit up all night anyway, you should try to interview that woman. She could give you a feel for what it's like to be a visitor at the prison on the day of an execution."

"Yeah, good idea," the man said. He thanked Trout, closed the door, and ran through the drizzle to catch the train.

To Trout's knowledge, the man never acted on the suggestion. Indeed, it was years later before he learned the identity of the woman he gave a ride to that night and realized the opportunity both he and the freshman reporter had missed.

Warden Buchanan sat down at Captain Rankin's desk, tore open the envelope Father Libs had handed him, and unfolded the enclosed letter flat on the blotter pad. It was composed in Tom Penney's distinctive handwriting on regulation prison stationery. The warden adjusted the desk lamp and read:

February 25, 1943

Dear Warden Buchanan,

By the time you read this you will have heard my final statement, and I can almost see the uncertainty in your eyes, just as I saw it that day in December when we met in confidence in your office. Despite your doubts at that meeting, and the anguish I detected that my revelations caused you, you kept that confidence.

In return, this letter is to provide you with the proof I believe you deserve that I did not lie to you that day, and that you have not executed an innocent man.

Why then, if Bob was guilty, did I change my testimony and try to get him sprung? Let me explain in terms I believe you will understand.

You are aware of the good works Father Donnelly did to bring me to the Holy Faith. Following my conversion I was overcome with remorse for the life I had led. The most difficult burden to bear was recognition of the years of grief I had caused my mother. While Bob and I were in jail in Lexington we could talk freely between our cells, and I shared those feelings with him. One day he told me he knew a way I could atone for the pain I had caused her. He said that if I would change my testimony and get him off, he would reopen the Cat and Fiddle and would share everything with my mother, equally. He said I should say that I had lied about him because of a fight we had over a liquor deal. He promised that if I did that, my mother would never want for another thing for as long as she lived, and he convinced me that there were ways to make his promise legally binding.

I thought about Bob's proposition for months. He renewed the offer frequently while we were in jail in Lexington. After we were transferred here to Eddyville we were never in close enough proximity for him to repeat it outright without being overhead. But he would allude to it from time to time—such as asking me about my mother's health—and I knew what he meant.

One day Bob had Captain Rankin bring me a page he had torn out of the Courier-Journal. Bob had circled a story about Buford Stewart being killed in a street brawl in Louisville. Stewart was a shady character and Bob kept calling out pointed questions to me: Hadn't Stewart and I been pals? Hadn't Stewart been my accomplice in some of my capers? Wasn't my pal Stewart just as mad as I had been about the falling out Bob and I had over that liquor deal? Bob and I had, indeed, had such an argument and there were witnesses to it. Bob's implication was clear. He was suggesting that I change my story and finger Stewart as my true accomplice and say I'd railroaded Bob for revenge.

It was an agonizing decision. But, right or wrong, I knew that Bob's offer was the only chance I had left to do something good for my mother. So, I made the deposition stating that Bob was innocent.

Willie (I will pay dearly in purgatory for that sin!) always felt personally responsible for Mrs. Miley's death and did not care what happened to him one way or another. He agreed to back up anything I said, and he did.

You'll recall the uproar my new statement made in the press. When Father Donnelly read about that he came to see me for what turned out to be the last time. That afternoon in my cell I confessed to him what I had done, and how I hoped it would give my mother a carefree life. He was not impressed. He told me that no matter how good my intentions were, I had lied myself into a trap. He pointed out that based on my new deposition, Bob would certainly get a new trial, and that I would have to repeat my accusations against Buford Stewart—under oath. This meant that I would be bearing false witness in the name of God at a time when I was on the threshold of meeting God face to face. It was then that I realized that I had been gambling with my soul.

I asked Father Donnelly if I should withdraw my deposition. He said no. He said that I had put myself in a position where no one would believe any further testimony I gave. He told me that if I would simply refuse to say anything further about the case, Bob most likely would not get a new trial. And that's what I decided to do, as you well know.

Now, why should you believe this, yet another version of my testimony? What I am about to reveal to you now I have told no one else, not even Father Donnelly. As far as I know, by the time you read this you will be the only person still alive who knows it.

On that terrible night in Lexington, after Bob shot Mrs. Miley and was pistol whipping her in the hallway, Marion Miley came out of her bedroom and knocked me down with a single blow. I was dazed, but still conscious. While I was lying on the floor I saw Bob shove his gun in Marion Miley's back and pull the trigger. She dropped at his feet, but she was still full of fight. When she fell to the floor she grabbed his leg and bit him with all the strength she had left. Bob screamed in pain. Then he reached down and grabbed her by the hair and shot her point-blank in the head. She was right next to me on the floor and her head exploded all over my face. I have had nightmares about it ever since. It nearly drove me insane and I tried to take my life several times, but I was a coward.

That bite was so deep that Bob had to staunch the blood with a handkerchief. That's why I had to drive when we fled the clubhouse. On the way back to Louisville I had to stop and tie a compress over Bob's wound. In jail in Lexington, and here in Eddyville, he would rub his leg and curse Marion Miley aloud. He never forgave her for that!

I'm sure the scar from that bite is still there, just above Bob's right ankle. And I've read enough about forensic pathology to know that it can be verified from Miss Miley's dental records, or, if need be, from her exhumed body. For that reason you can be assured that what I am writing now is the truth, for I am not about to die with a lie on my soul.

Now I must close. Soon you will be coming to see me for the final time in this life. I thank you for being aboveboard with me all the way, and may God bless you and grant you peace.

At the right of the Holy Cross,
Tom Penney

Warden Buchanan laid the letter on the desk and sat back.

At the right of the Holy Cross?

The meaning finally came to him. *Dismas*—Penney's favorite Biblical character. Tradition held that the penitent criminal at the crucifixion died on the cross to the right of Jesus Christ.

27

The prison yard was dark, illuminated by only a few widely spaced street lights and the floods that lighted the walls. Five minutes after reading Tom Penney's letter, the warden was walking across the vacant yard en route to the hospital. Almost at once he was joined by two well-groomed German Shepherd dogs, Black Girl and Queenie, who stayed at his heels. The dogs were kept in special shelters during the day and released only at night. They had been trained to recognize the warden's scent and those of other prison officials who required access to the prison yard after darkness. But woe be to anyone they encountered whose scent they did not recognize.

At the hospital the warden sent his canine escorts on other rounds and entered the prison morgue. A cavernous, brightly lighted room, the morgue reeked this night of formaldehyde.

Alongside one wall, three simple pine boxes lay waiting to receive the bodies of the executed men. They would be dressed in prison-made suits and shipped home or buried at state expense in the remote cemetery behind the prison as their families desired.

In the center of the room Mortician Samuel Glenn was laying out instruments beside a bare ceramic table. Glenn, a distinguished silver-haired man in private practice, looked up. "Warden . . . you startled me."

"Sorry, Sam. Go on with your work."

Nearby, three sheet-covered bodies lay on separate gurneys. Glenn had already re-shaped the rigid angle at which the men's legs had been fused during electrocution, and all the bodies lay flat. The warden lifted the sheet covering the short, chunky body of Bob Anderson and looked closely at the right ankle. He frowned. The flesh was discolored from the high-voltage electrode that had been strapped there. He looked closer.

"Sam, can you spare a minute?"

The mortician stepped over to the gurney. The warden pointed. "That mark right there . . . what do you think it is?"

The mortician leaned down and peered for several seconds at the barely visible cicatrix on Bob's leg, just above the ankle. "I can tell you exactly what it is, Warden. It's a scar."

"Well, hell, Sam, I know that. What kind of scar?"

"It's a bite mark."

"Human?"

"No doubt about it."

"Now, Sam, are you certain?"

"Well I ought to be," Sam Glenn replied testily. "I've seen enough of them."

"I'm sure you have." The warden softened his tone. "Can you tell me how old it is?"

The mortician studied the scar again, probing and stretching the flesh for several seconds. "A year, maybe. No more that two. Why? Is it important?"

The warden put the sheet back in place. "Yes, very important. Thank you, Sam."

The warden lifted the sheet from the tallest figure and

looked at Tom Penney's face. It was more peaceful than he had ever seen it. He replaced the sheet and looked toward the gurney bearing the smallest figure. Willie Baxter's body lay almost lost beneath the draping folds, as insignificant in death as he had been in life. Poor Willie. Executed for the crime of poverty and ignorance.

The warden left the morgue and walked back across the prison yard to the administration building. He entered his office, switched on the lights, and went to his desk. He locked Tom's letter in a drawer. It was state's evidence. After-the-fact, but evidence nonetheless. He would deliver it personally to the state attorney general at the next opportunity.

Weary, his mind filled with conflicting emotions, he sat back in deep reflection. It had been a climactic day. The most sensational murders in Kentucky's history had been avenged.

Or had they?

Could any death avenge another? he wondered. He thought of the three men whose executions were so fresh in his mind. One defiant, one contrite, and . . . Willie. He recalled Senator Barkley's words: "Only the helpless hang."

He thought of Tom Penney's letter: " . . . to provide you with the proof I believe you deserve that . . . you have not executed an innocent man." What if Penney had not written that final absolving letter this fateful night? What of other nights to come?

He sat forward, pulled his IN basket to him, and rummaged through it. Near the bottom he found what he was looking for. The neatly typed letter to Senator McKellar, ready for signature, stating that the warden was honored to have been asked, but he felt he could not support the senator's penal reform bill. He read the letter through, then took a pen and boldly marked a huge *X* across the face of it. At the bottom he wrote: "Henry, please re-type. Tell the senator that I will, indeed, support his bill and will testify on its behalf at any time."

Though he didn't realize it at the time, Warden Buchanan had just taken the first step in what would become a lifelong crusade.

He went to the outer office and dropped the letter onto Henry Sproule's desk as the first order of business to attend to later that morning. He looked at his watch: 1:35 A.M. From the distance came the whistle of the eastbound Illinois Central passenger train signaling for a stop at Kuttawa to pick up Louisville-bound customers. He listened for a moment, then switched off the lights, walked across the hallway, and climbed the stairs to his apartment.

He had four hours left for sleep before he'd have to rise to face a new prison day.

Epilogue

During his seventeen-year tenure at the Kentucky State Penitentiary, Warden W. Jesse Buchanan supervised the execution of fifty-one men. For many years, he performed this service in the spirit of duty. However, the execution of the Milley murderers profoundly affected him and proved to be crucial in altering the course of capital punishment in America. Following his retirement in 1955 Jesse Buchanan became an indefatigable spokesman for the abolition of capital punishment, not only stressing the barbarity of the act but also emphasizing the dehumanizing effect it has on those who must carry out the sentence. Acknowledged as one whose opinions were based on hard experience rather than conjecture, he was widely sought as a speaker on the subject. He appeared before numerous state and federal legislative and judicial bodies, as well as interested private groups, whose views encompassed both sides of the question.

237

Though he did not live to see the result of his crusade, his involvement was instrumental in bringing about the ten-year moratorium on capital punishment that prevailed in the United States until the execution of Gary Gilmore in Utah in 1977.

"On the issue of capital punishment," U.S. Chief Justice Fred Vinson once remarked, "no person in our time is more entitled to a respectful audience than Jess Buchanan."

Warden Buchanan died on March 6, 1962. When news of his death reached the state capital in Frankfort, the Kentucky House of Representatives adjourned in honor of his memory.

About the Author

William J. Buchanan is the author of six books, including the bestseller *A Shining Season*, which became a CBS Television Movie of the Week. The son of Warden Jesse Buchanan, he became interested in the Miley case and spent hours in Kentucky State Penitentiary interviewing the condemned men. From these interviews, interviews with his father (plus his father's private notes), and those with others involved in the case, he gained a unique perspective on the case. The author is an Adjunct Professor of Creative Writing at the University of New Mexico, and he resides in Albuquerque.